PSYCHIC PETS

Emma Heathcote-James

PSYCHIC PETS

HOW ANIMAL INTUITION AND PERCEPTION HAS CHANGED HUMAN LIVES

JOHN BLAKE

Published by John Blake Publishing Ltd,
3 Bramber Court, 2 Bramber Road,
London W14 9PB, England

www.blake.co.uk

First published in hardback in 2007

ISBN 978 1 84454 357 1

British Library Cataloguing-in-Publication Data:

A catalogue record for this book is available from the British Library.

Design by www.envydesign.co.uk

Printed in Great Britain by William Clowes Ltd, Beccles, Suffolk

1 3 5 7 9 10 8 6 4 2

Papers used by John Blake Publishing Ltd are natural, recyclable
products made from wood grown in sustainable forests. The
manufacturing processes conform to the environmental regulations of
the country of origin.

Every attempt has been made to contact the relevant copyright-
holders, but some were unobtainable. We would be grateful if the
appropriate people could contact us.

Through the centuries, dogs and other animals have
shown their dedication to mankind in a variety of ways.
Some have exhibited courage in extreme situations, others,
by total dedication and affection to their owners.
The following compilation is but a small number of those
instances that deserve our respect, admiration and gratitude.
This book is dedicated to all loyal pets, registered assistance
animals and their charities. Not forgetting, of course,
my very own special four legged friend, Mr Mutley.

Other books by the author
Seeing Angels
After-Death Communication
They Walk Among Us

'A superb and easy-to-read book. A true gem… full of compelling evidence… it may change how you live your life.'
After Death Communication Research Foundation,
Tacoma, Washington

'A thoughtful intelligent contribution… on a very important subject. It cannot fail to stimulate enquiring minds everywhere.'
Society for Psychical Research on *After DeathCommunication*

'Hundreds of compelling stories – an astonishing number of people believe they have communicated with loved ones.'
Daily Mail on *After Death Communication*

'No doubt Emma's book will inspire many people, primarily because of its simplicity. It speaks directly to one's heart…'
Bill and Judy Guggenheim, The ADC Project and co-authors of *Hello from Heaven!* on *After Death Communication*'

After Death Communication – that's the title of a new book on spirit communication that will shortly be winging its way across the Atlantic… many have felt it best to keep these things to themselves for fear of being ridiculed or dismissed as indulging in wishful thinking. But why are people treated as odd for speaking of the experience asks Heathcote-James, if one in three of us has them?'
The Parapsychic Journal

'*After Death Communication* is thoroughly researched and beautifully written with the scientific mind and lovingly spiritual heart of Emma Heathcote-James. It's a truly comforting book for those who've experienced an After Death Communication, and for those who wonder about life after death.'

Doreen Virtue, Ph.D, author of countless books, CDs and oracle cards (Hay House)

'It's life's biggest mystery: Can we survive the grave? So why is science ignoring it?'

Daily Mail on *They Walk Among Us*

Foreword

Without doubt, the wind of change is blowing in all areas of mind, body and spirit. From a mere zephyr a decade ago, to the gale we are experiencing today, people all over the world are more than happy to talk about spiritual experiences of every kind, leading to an acceptance of a psycho-spiritual element in animals. In the ten years I have been researching and writing about the paranormal – mainly in relation to angels – I have noticed more and more stories reaching me about the spiritual aspect of animals.

From the dawn of time, animals have been important to mankind, not just for their ability to work for man, but also for their close relationship to humans. Indigenous peoples had a deep respect for animals and a keen understanding of their qualities and psychic abilities. As society becomes more sophisticated, however, it looses the once simple ability to communicate on a deeper level with animals. Ancient Egyptians literally worshiped their cats, recognising what amazing creatures they were and strived to communicate with them on a daily basis. In the Middle Ages, cats were often associated with witchcraft and special powers, inducing fear in the general population. Could this stem from the fact that the so-called 'witch' happened to be on the same wavelength as their pets? The old cliché 'use it or loose it' certainly rings true – it is time we began to plug in to these special and readily-available powers to communicate with our pets.

It is a well-known and recognised fact that animals are super sensitive. Numerous natural history programmes on television today underline this fact. Pictures of elephants for instance, mourning the loss of a partner or offspring, bring tears to ones' eyes on seeing such overwhelming tenderness and empathy; dolphins displaying the near-human ability to communicate with one another; and also the family bonds of the great apes. I recall the story related in the national press some years ago, of a young boy falling into a gorilla enclosure, where he lay unconscious on the pit floor. His distraught mother and horrified onlookers watched as a huge female gorilla approached the limp little body. Far from harming the boy, however, she gently stood watch and kept more boisterous gorillas at bay until the keeper could reach the child. Such sensitivity is a mere step away from the psychic ability recorded in these pages.

Emma Heathcote-James has researched her subject with admirable thoroughness, covering many aspects of animal behaviour with stories that leave one simply astonished. We are all familiar with accounts of people suffering bereavement and declaring that their pet 'understands and displays love and affection in abundance at such times'. However, this book goes beyond such familiar and everyday accounts to give a comprehensive overview of the remarkable psychic ability of the animal kingdom. This book will inspire you to tune in and discover your pets in a totally different light. Whether whispering to a horse or feeling a close bond of love with a tiny pet rabbit, the ability to communicate psychically is clearly possible. On reading this book, sceptics may find their lack of belief wavering, for it cannot fail to touch us on a deeply spiritual level. Uplifting and heart-warming, *Psychic Pets* will inspire and alter our attitude to pets forever.

Glennyce S Eckersley,
author of *Angel Awakenings*

Preface

'Until one has loved an animal, a part of one's soul remains unawakened.'

ANATOLE FRANCE

Living and breathing organisms often demonstrate a so-called sixth sense – a power of perception beyond the normal five senses. Call it intuition, an inner voice, a psychic power or vibes, animals and humans share this capacity to respond to their environments in ways we know little about. Animals instinctively know how to live and what they need – birds migrate, some mammals hibernate, they can anticipate danger, know what to eat and are aware of changing weather. The majority of we humans have all our basic needs met and have consequently forgotten to listen to our bodies and inner voice. The animals have not – and this is why we have so much to learn from them.

It wasn't until I started researching for this book that I

realised the huge role animals play in our lives, even if we are not fully aware of their impact. Whether they help us through an emotionally difficult time, bring us joy or physically rescue us, pets can not only be our best friends, but lifesavers, too. Of course, I had heard of Guide Dogs for the Blind and Hearing Dogs but I wasn't aware of the vast role played by Support Dogs, Dogs for the Disabled or the incredible Seizure Alert Dogs. It is not just dogs – did you know that 10,000 cats are 'employed' by the British Government to keep official buildings rodent free? Or the extent to which all animals have been, and still are being, used in war?

Every single day there are countless occurrences of animals helping us to live our lives to the full. These animals consistently, compassionately and courageously use their awareness to aid humans – some do this as part of their special training, others act out of sheer natural instinct to look after their human friends or an instinct for survival from disasters. Acts range from the simple opening of a door for a disabled owner to something as dramatic as saving lives or bringing love and affection to those in real need. No matter what the deed, though, down the centuries animals have shown their true kindness, bravery, perseverance and devotion.

Animals just seem 'to know', and for centuries the unconditional bond and love that pets have given their owners has been documented, but rarely has it been seen as a cause for real acknowledgement. *Psychic Pets* highlights the ceaseless and unselfish contributions that animals have made, and continue to make, to our lives. This book is a collection of accounts, stories and facts to show all the incredible things that our animal friends do, and have done, to aid and enhance our lives. Anyone who has a pet or who works with animals knows of the human-animal bond. Pet owners will explain how, 'Rover knows exactly what I'm saying – he understands every word', and while the sceptics claim it's just tone of voice or body language that they are responding to, I don't think it really matters – I have experienced and read about too many instances of this bond. My angle here is that there is unequivocally and irrevocably a telepathic bond between man and beast. For the sake of argument, I will call this 'telepathy'.

A huge shift in our attitudes towards the whole mind, body, spirit genre is taking place. As a nation we are turning to alternative therapies as never before, for drugs are no longer seen as the only answer. We accept that disease often stems from the mind, albeit in some cases subconsciously. In place of processed and chemically-infested foods, we are choosing purer, more nutritionally balanced products, and an ever-increasing number of people recognise the mind, body, spirit connection. It is as we acknowledge this new awareness that we can learn from our animal friends.

So, *Psychic Pets* begins by looking at the age-old question 'Are Pets Psychic or Just Super-Sensitive?' It delves into the idea of a sixth sense and the relationship between humans and animals. Chapter 2 continues to explore their natural instinct by considering recent research into the idea of animals being early detectors of anything ranging from earthquakes, tornados and other natural occurrences with a proven track record. Chapter 3 expands on this and looks at animal superstitions, such as whether they can predict the weather, with Chapter 4 looking at dogs as working partners, such as police sniffer dogs, military and rescue dogs, while Chapter 5 explores the abilities of Guide Dogs for the Blind, Hearing Dogs for deaf people, Dogs for the Disabled and Seizure Alert Dogs (the Epilepsy Institute says that dogs can be trained to tell when a person is about to have a seizure and Seizure Alert Dogs are trained to look after their epileptic owners, steering them to safety before a fit so that if they fall they don't get hurt).

Chapter 6 investigates special stories of animals in war and Chapter 7 takes the idea a step further by offering many instances around us which show us that pets have qualities which we can harness. For example, PAT (Pets as Therapy) animals and CHATA (Children in Hospital and Animal Therapy Association) show the exceptional therapeutic qualities animals provide and I examine the report of the *British Medical Journal* on the ability of dogs to sniff out cancerous tumours. Chapter 8 looks at life-saving animals, whether they have helped their own kind or humans, while Chapter 9 celebrates famous animals around the world who have touched our lives. Finally, Chapter 10 explores pets returning from the grave in Animal After Death Communication.

EJH-J
North Cotswolds

Acknowledgements

Again, this book isn't totally down to me – it is a culmination of a lot of enthusiasm and support from many different people and organisations who believed the timing of this book was ready, needed and achievable. Of course, first and foremost thanks to my parents and little brother for their ongoing support,and to the Aussie side of the family who all patiently put up with me finishing off the manuscript, and finally to all those below who helped make this book possible.

To John and Rosie, as always, for believing in this; thanks for such a lovely relationship over what has become a number of years. And in turn to Clive and all at John Blake for turning this around!

To Rupert Sheldrake, whose groundbreaking exploration of animal behaviour was such an inspiration.

To all the Registered Assistance charities and animal therapy organisations, including:

- Maureen Hennis and volunteers at Pets As Therapy (PAT), including Claire Taylor for providing assistance with the 'Effects of brief Pets as Therapy visits on mood state in nursing homes and day centres' study, along with Jane Ambler (PAT dogs Bonaparte, Cognac and Jamey) and Catherine Corey (PAT dog Boone)
- Chris Dyson and the Guide Dogs' Communications Department
- Jenny Moir and Gill Lacey at Hearing Dogs
- Rebecca Bell and Kym Stretton at Seizure Alert Dogs
- Sarah Watson at Dogs for Disabled
- Hannah Taylor at Support Dogs
- Sergeant Jennings at the Dog Training Unit, Borsel Common for West Midlands Police
- The volunteers of Children in Hospital and Animal Therapy Association (CHATA)
- The Zoological Society London, and Kim Riley at Twycross Zoo
- Margaret Bramell, Mr Mutley's local co-ordinator
- The staff and residents of the Four Seasons in Chipping Campden

To my fantastic publicist, Ailsa Macalister, for enlisting the press in helping me source stories. To everyone who has helped us via print, sound or television, especially Sophie Marsh and the BBC Local Channel, Katie Johnson at BBC H&W, Tony Donnely at the *Evesham* and *Cotswold Journal*, BBC Humberside, BBC Newcastle, BBC West Midlands, BBC Manchester, BBC Kent, BBC Northampton and BBC Belfast, who all featured this book on various shows, doing phone-ins and helping me collect accounts and stories to fill these pages.

To Marianne Rankin and The Alistair Hardy Research Centre and the North Cotswold Group for your time, understanding and welcome lunches!

To Julian Drewitt, Val Baker, Sylvia Hickman, Sarah Dicks and the Worcester and Cheltenham Branches of Churches Fellowship for Psychical and Spiritual Studies (CFPSS) for your time, support, articles and letters.

To Kate Henderson for your interest and help in sourcing and passing on relevant articles, and all connected to the GMG and the University of Gloucestershire.

To my friends, as always to Glennyce Eckersley for just being, understanding and knowing you are there! Gay Pilgrim for listening to my tangents and telling me off whenever it was needed! To Linda and Huw Meads for your recent friendship and time, to Dan Howard, Susan Henderson, Cathy Haslem and to all the usuals – John Bluck, Big Nigel, Mr Darcy, Lily Harwood, Kathy Carmichael, Kate and Richard Miles, Alix West and Pete, and all the others, to save a long list you know who you are! And then, last but not least, to all my wonderful neighbours, especially Rob and Helen Davis, the Wheatleys, the Applebys and everyone else. We are so fortunate to live in such a special place. Thank you for everything you have done and continue to do.

And last, but by no means least, to Mr Mutley – thank you for refusing to be a gun dog and thus introducing me to the world of animal-assisted therapy. I hope I give you back as much as you have done to enhance and enrich my life and all those who you touch. And that extends to all the incredible animals who deserve a world of admiration – as the sixteenth-century playwright Ben Jonson once wrote, 'I do honour the very flea of his dog'.

Contents

Introduction

'Mummy! Mummy!' shouted Chloe running in excitedly from school. She ran into the living room where her mother was sitting. She was so excited, she could hardly catch her breath, but eventually she got the words out. 'You can get a dog! There are dogs that help people like you and do lots of clever things – they can pick up the telephone, open doors and take your coat off.'

Hayley Rayner of Chatteris, in Cambridgeshire, was a little bewildered to say the least by her daughter's sudden idea, but gradually the penny dropped. Hayley remembered a television programme that the family had watched over Christmas, as she explained, 'There was a programme featuring a dog that helped a boy in a wheelchair with the things that he found difficult to do. Chloe was really impressed and thought that I could get a dog like that. She just kept on and on about it. I couldn't believe my eyes and thought it was camera trickery. I told

Chloe that dogs couldn't really do things like that, otherwise everyone would want one!'

Chloe, then aged 8, had other ideas and the thought of a dog to help her mum just kept on coming up in her mind. Returning to school after the holidays, the first thing she did was to ask her teacher to help her on the Internet and, there it was, a charity that trained dogs to assist disabled people. At last she had found a way to help her mum. Now Hayley was also intrigued by the idea of how a dog could help. 'Having a look at the website, I began to feel hopeful and share some of Chloe's excitement. She had been right – there were people like me that had dogs to help them.'

Hayley had been diagnosed with multiple sclerosis only five weeks after the birth of her son, Alex. From that moment on, life for the whole family was turned upside down. Over the next six years, Hayley gradually discovered that every element of her life would be affected: her muscles were weakened, she had poor balance, making it difficult to do anything – from looking after her new-born baby to picking up the post – and she also developed a tremor which, combined with her balance and muscle weakness, meant that she could easily drop anything that she picked up.

'The following day,' said Hayley, 'I picked up the phone to see if Dogs for the Disabled could help me.' It was about a year before she was contacted by the charity to say that they had a match. A home visit introduced her to Uska and from that moment on, things began to look up. 'Uska walked in the door and I just knew that he'd be part of my life.'

A two-week residential course at the charity's centre in Banbury, in Oxfordshire, gave Hayley the tools that she required to look after Uska and helped to establish the unique and unbreakable bond which is formed between a disabled person and their assistance dog. She learnt every aspect of Uska's care and how to get him to do the tasks that she needed help with. By the time they headed home, Hayley felt excited for the future. Uska had already started to bond with her and was helping with basic tasks, such as picking up Hayley's keys or purse, and opening doors for her.

Hayley continues:

> 'Until I got home with Uska, I don't think I'd realised just how much confidence I'd lost since I became disabled. Having Uska has helped to reverse some of those feelings. When you become disabled, you lose all your independence. You don't expect to get it back, but having Uska did exactly that. I have gained some of the freedom I'd lost. Uska's great: he helps me to empty the washing machine, he can open doors and he'll fetch my shoes, or a jacket. He comes to the shops now and it's great because together we can do some shopping and be on our way – I don't need to ask people to help me so much.'

The family has noticed the difference with Uska around: Chloe and Alex love him, but Hayley's husband Alistair says he didn't expect an Assistance Dog to be such a great help for everyone. 'I didn't know having an assistance dog would make such a difference to the whole family. Hayley goes out now because she feels more confident. Being in a wheelchair can put people off speaking to a person. I don't think people know how to react, but when people see Uska they just want to find out more, so they start to talk to Hayley.' It has also helped Alistair and the family feel more positive. 'I've been amazed how much more I can relax when I go out. I don't need to make sure Hayley has everything she needs now, as I know Uska can get it for her, if she needs it. You always worry that if anything should happen, Hayley wouldn't be able to get help, but with Uska around I know he'll raise the alarm. It's great for Chloe and her brother Alex as well, because it means that they can play and know that Uska's there to help their mum.'[1]

Animals – be they working, assistance dogs, run-of-the-mill pets or even wild creatures – can have a monumental impact on our lives. They have the amazing ability to fulfil the most basic human needs: love, affection, companionship and, yes, even survival. Their positive influence can have a profound effect on our everyday lives and this book aims to capture some personal stories of how they have enriched human lives. Animals are being used in the detection of disease, relief of stress, and as communication vehicles for those with learning difficulties, as support to the disabled and as therapists to the sick, to name but a few uses.

British mythology depicts the dog as a faithful and loyal companion. It serves its master well and is prepared to defend that person to the death. King Arthur's faithful companion Cabal is but one dog that symbolises the relationship between humans and dogs that has survived through the centuries. Like us, animals are purely spiritual beings but differ immensely in their qualities of unconditional love, healing, forgiveness, patience, courage and gratitude – virtues that are often lacking in our modern materialistic high-tech, yet low-touch, lives.

1 Taken from *Newshound* and reproduced by permission of Dogs for the Disabled

In this age of ecological emergency, more and more people are realising the need to recognise their oneness and connection with all living beings. Communication and the bond between humans and animals have taken on a deeper meaning and with a sense of urgency. There is so much that we can learn from animals about how to live in harmony and balance on the Earth… a basic which is certainly lacking in early twenty-first-century living.

THE BENEFITS OF BEING A PET OWNER

Britain is a nation of animal lovers with, at the last count, over seven million of us owning a dog and half a million more a cat. It has been estimated that just over half of all the households in England have a pet, the most common being a dog, cat, bird or fish. We all know the many physical benefits that pets confer on people no matter what their age: pets offer a sense of wellbeing, a sense of encouragement and, for some, even a reason for living. Pets help people of all ages to learn about responsibility, loyalty, empathy, sharing and unconditional love – qualities particularly essential to us as a race. Through caring for a pet, we also learn to care for our fellow human beings. There is an established link between how people treat animals and how they treat each other. Kindness to animals is a lesson that benefits people, too. Ask anyone with a pet or a love of animals what it is about them that they feel so drawn to. Animals have a known calming quality; they are dependent on us and enrich our lives far beyond anything that words can describe.

A researcher called Bolin cited by the Pets as Therapy charity found that people who owned pets were less likely to experience depression than those who did not. Wilson and Turner[2] also suggested that pets are beneficial in reducing anxiety and depression as they offer unconditional love and attention; they make people laugh, help them to relax and offer diversion from day-to-day concerns.

McNicholas and Collins[3] suggested a support model of pets. They stated that pets are perceived as always available, predictable in their responses and non-judgemental and suggested that they provide a sense of esteem in that pets are perceived as both caring about their owners and needing them, regardless of the owners' status as perceived by themselves and others. Pets can also give tactile comfort and recreational distraction from worries. Wilson also found that owning a pet reduces anxiety. He suggested that pets might act as buffers to stress, helping their owners to cope with stress and anxiety, which may also lead to lower levels of depression in pet owners.[4]

Research definitely backs up our yearning to share our lives with these furry creatures – studies at the University of New York, in Buffalo, found that pet owners in general have a lower resting heart rate and blood pressure than those who don't keep animals; and recovery rate from stress is significantly quicker than non-pet owners. One could go so far as stating that pets might even help prevent marriage breakdowns. Another study

2 Wilson, C. C. and Turner, D. C., *Companion Animals in Human Health*. Sage Publications, 1998

3 1995, cited in Wilson and Turner, 1998

4 Study findings of the effects of brief Pets As Therapy visits on mood state in nursing homes and day

at Buffalo revealed that pet-owning couples had closer relationships and were more satisfied with their marriages!

Interestingly, a survey by Douglas Davis's[5] revealed that 55 per cent of dog owners and 44 per cent of cat owners celebrated their pets' birthdays; that 77 per cent of respondents' cats slept on their owners' beds, as did 48 per cent of respondents' dogs. Approximately 80 per cent of these pet owners were aware of the anniversary of their pets' death. Practically all talked to their pets and also regarded their pets as members of the family.

It is possible to analyse the strength of feeling that some owners have for their pets by asking them what sort of status they believe their pet has in the family unit. The results were as follows:

Equal adult members of the family: 19% (dogs) 23% (cats)
Junior members of the family: 25% (dogs) 25% (cats)
Animal members of the family: 54% (dogs) 51% (cats)

As one respondent to this book replied, 'Our dogs are part of our family. Owning animals is a joy, but also a responsibility. Our dogs are spoilt, they cuddle up to us on the sofas and sleep on our bed at night. My mother doesn't approve, but they are a big part of our lives. I hesitate to say our babies.'

The significance we give our pets gives them a special raised status in family life and in our way of viewing them. To the sceptic, we personify them, imagining their thoughts and feelings, making them into beings they simply are not... whether you believe this is up to you.

5 Davies, Douglas, pp170–1, *Death, Ritual and Belief*, Cassell, London, 1997

ANIMALS AND HUMANS: INTELLECT, FEELINGS AND MEMORY

Animals have been an intrinsic part of human life for as long has history as been recorded. However, the idea of mutual respect and fealty waivered with western philosopy, as it struggled to understand man's place in the world. In the seventeenth century, Descartes expressed the opinion that since animals do not speak our language, they must lack reason and souls. He famously stated that 'the reason why animals do not speak as we do is not that they lack the organs but that they have no thoughts'. Descartes obviously never considered the possibility of non-verbal language, nor the emotional bond so familiar to every owner, carer and handler.

Since then, others have joined the debate (with the same negative view), more recently claiming the only way to study scientifically the psychology of animals was through their behaviour. Burrhus Skinner, an American behaviourist and psychologist gave his name to the Skinner Box, a simple machine to train rats and pigeons to respond to stimuli. Essentially, it was a device to test 'simple machines' as if animals are machines, without feelings, thoughts or consciousness and, if their only role to mankind is to be useful, then it doesn't really matter what we do with them so long as we utilise them to their full potential! The outrages of factory farming, live animal exports, battery hens, force-feeding ducks and geese for foie gras and so forth are a logical result of such a point of view.

For a long time, animal behaviourists were only interested in studying responses to external stimuli – anyone interested in what animals did of their own accord and spontaneously was labelled a hopeless romantic! However, as we know, animals are more than machines, such as a computer which we can merely programme and train to do what we want. They are, like us, intelligent beings capable of learning by themselves – tests upon tests have proven this, such as squirrels obliging researchers by tackling the most intricate obstacle courses to reach a dish of peanuts that display problem solving techniques which in turn require thought, memory and, of course, intelligence.[6]

An incredible account was sent to me from Hearing Dogs. Anyone who has been stung by a wasp knows just how painful it can be and is probably wary of the insects in the future. However, Roddy, a young hearing dog, has employed his own methods of dealing with them!

Roddy, a tan and white Papillon, was donated to the national charity, Hearing Dogs for Deaf People, when he was four months old. After being socialised with one of the charity's volunteers, he came into the training centre in Buckinghamshire for sixteen weeks' advanced soundwork training. As part of this training, he was taught to respond to everyday household sounds, such as the doorbell and telephone, by touching his trainer to alert her and then leading her back to the source of the sound.

Towards the end of his training, Roddy was unfortunately stung by a wasp and had a very severe allergic reaction, which resulted in him collapsing and he was rushed to the vet for emergency life-saving treatment. It was touch and go for a

6 Ball, S. and Howard, J., Ch. 1, The Background, pp 2–3, *Bach Flower Remedies for Animals*, Vermillion, London, 2005

while, but Roddy recovered and successfully completed his training, and went to live with his deaf recipient, Doreen Amos, who lives in Somerset.

One day, not long after he moved in with Doreen, Roddy rushed to her and started scrabbling at her, which is his way of alerting her to something going on. When Doreen asked him, 'What is it?' Roddy led her back to his dog bed and Doreen immediately saw that there was a wasp buzzing around his bedding. As soon as Doreen disposed of the insect, Roddy happily curled up in his bed and went to sleep!

Although hearing dogs are trained to respond to sounds, Roddy not only worked out that it was a wasp that had hurt him in the past, but used his initiative and Hearing Dog training to alert his owner and ask her to remove the problem!

So, if animals are capable of intelligent thought and rely on more than instinct to survive, then it is no step at all to assume that they must also have the capacity to feel emotions and have individual personalities of their own?

As Glennyce refers to in the foreword, there is a distressing story about a cow elephant dying in a safari park, that implies grief on the part of an elephant mate. This was told by Bruce Fogle in his book *The Dog's Mind*. The pathologist decided to carry out a post mortem on the large dead animal and, because of the difficulty in moving it, decided to do the examination on the spot where it had died.

As the work got underway, the pathologist needed help to move the large, dismembered pieces around the shed. A bull elephant, the dead cow's mate, was brought in to help him shift them. First, it was made to pick up and move one of the legs, which it did, although it seemed agitated. Then it had to move the cow's head – again, it did as it was told, but beat its trunk in the air and trumpeted once it had done so. After this the door was opened and the elephant allowed to leave. It ran outside and as far away as possible from the shed, pressed its head onto the ground and trumpeted for a long time. Until its trainer came up and spoke to it, it did not move again.

The fact is that the brains of all mammals – including our own and an elephant's –are so similar it is simpler to hypothesise that animals do have emotions than it is to deny their existence. This means that Occam's razor, a respected scientific principle that prefers the simpler of two theories, supports the unscientific belief that we can, and should understand this elephant's pain.[7]

Similar to this is Katie's account – she wrote to me about a time she was milking the cows. She had them all in the holding pen ready for milking, and one of the female cows dropped dead with a heart attack: 'I went out to see what the noise was – of course, the noise of a cow falling on the ground is quite noisy, but what was strange was how the other girls responded. It was very quiet and very respectful; their behaviour totally changed, as if they could tell and were definitely moved. It really was quite eerie.'

I recall a similar occasion when helping a friend out at sheep-shearing time – the stress of the sheep being herded into holding pens, then gradually fed into a single track 'route' leading to the turnstile where they are taken and sheared proved too much for one ewe, who collapsed while being shorn and died a few minutes later – again, with a heart attack. The

---

7 Ball, S. and Howard, J., p 10, *Bach Flower Remedies for Animals*, Vermillion, London, 2005

atmosphere among the others who had already been shorn in the big pen around the clippers was apparent. They 'knew' what was going on.

Another time, I remember walking around a reservoir in Birmingham and seeing a dead female duck in the water with its male companion circling it – if animals are purely given to survival instinct, then such behaviour doesn't make sense at all.

To sum up, I think we all know in our hearts that animals have feelings, emotions and memories – think of dogs lying in front of the fire with their legs twitching and 'running' as they dream of the day's walk and sniffs – the rapid eye movement (REM) rates of dreaming dogs can be measured to prove this, too. Cats also become distinctly unsettled when taken to a new house. At the end of the day, scientists are still unable to measure human emotion satisfactorily, so animals' emotions are even further down the list to investigate thoroughly in the science labs!

CHAPTER 1

Are Pets Psychic or Just Super-Sensitive?

'Lots of people talk to animals… Not very many listen, though… That's the problem.'

THE TAO OF POOH, BENJAMIN HOFF

Ask any dog or cat owner and they will vouch for their animal's acute senses, especially for impending storms, family members' illnesses and moods, knowing when a family member is due home, or when returning home from unfamiliar journeys or, indeed, knowing when they were almost near to their destination in the car. Maybe it is down to smells, vibrations and perhaps recognising local sounds that our ears are unable to filter. Whatever the answer, are they 'psychic', super-sensitive, or do the two equate to the same thing?

We've all heard the stories:

• a pet cat jumps up onto the windowsill every day, several minutes before its owner arrives home

1

- a pet dog barks just before a certain person calls on the phone, as if knowing the call was being made
- a pet parrot, who's learnt to talk, says things seemingly in response to what its owner is thinking
- a beloved pet, somehow lost on a family trip, miraculously finds its way home – sometimes travelling hundreds, or even thousands, of miles

Are they remarkable stories of animal telepathy, or their sense of direction and premonition, or are they examples of animals' keen senses, or evidence of an unexplained psychic ability?

How are these things possible? Do our pets – perhaps even all animals – possess some innate psychic ability that allows them to tune in to human brainwaves, or even to see the future? Or are they just more sensitive than humans to visual, aural, magnetic and other subtle environmental factors and changes – and thus, because we are not aware of these subtleties, their actions seem miraculous? It's an ongoing debate, usually with the psychically minded and a lot of devoted pet owners on one side, and the more sceptical and scientifically minded on the other.

After publishing articles and pleas for help in numerous newspapers and veterinary surgeries, zoos and safari parks, as well as animal-related magazines, the question – I believe – has been answered by the amazing personal experiences outlined throughout this book, all stating that their beloved pets and animals do indeed seem to exhibit a sensitivity to things unseen, or a psychic connection to another world.

As with all my other work, the problem of language and all connotations ascribed to a word come into play. 'Psychic' perhaps isn't the best word to use, as it conjures up images of crystal balls and Mystic Meg. Maybe, we should simply state that animals are, rather incredibly, 'super sensitive'. Pets seem to have the amazing ability to sense what we cannot and, in ways that we don't understand, to communicate with us, perhaps even after death. Animals appear to have a more finely tuned sixth sense than humans and the fact they possess such skills which cannot be explained rationally has inevitably lead them to be called psychic.

A survey was carried out by telephone in London to find out how any pet owners had observed seemingly telepathic abilities in their pets. Fifty-two per cent of dog owners claimed their animals knew in advance when a member of the household was on the way home, compared with 24 per cent of cat owners. Of the animals that reacted, 21 per cent of dogs and 19 per cent of cats were said to do so more than ten minutes before the person's return. Seventy-three per cent of dog owners and 52 per cent of cat owners said their pets knew when the owners were going out before they showed any signs of doing so; 43 per cent of dog owners and 41 per cent of cat owners said their pets responded to their thoughts or silent commands and 57 per cent of dog owners and 37 per cent of cat owners said their pets were sometimes telepathic with them. Forty-six per cent of people currently with pets and 37 per cent of people currently without pets said that they had known pets in the past that were telepathic. Thirty-nine per cent of those currently owning pets and 38 per cent of those currently without pets said they themselves had had psychic experiences. But significantly fewer of those who had never kept pets had had psychic experiences themselves. The results of this survey are compared with two similar surveys in the north-west of England and in California. The general pattern was remarkably similar in these three very different locations and shows that seemingly telepathic abilities in pets are common. In all locations, dogs were more responsive than cats to their owners' thoughts and intentions. The potential for experimental investigations of these abilities has already been discussed in the scientific community.[1]

Harvard and Cambridge biochemist, Dr Rupert Sheldrake, author of *Dogs That Know When Their Owners Are Coming Home* (Arrow, London, 2000) is the expert in this field. He believes animals have abilities that humans may have possessed at one time, but somehow lost. Through his extensive research, he has concluded that there are three major categories of unexplained perceptiveness by animals:

1. Telepathy – a psychic connection that some pets may have with their owners through connections Sheldrake calls 'morphic fields'. It is this ability that enables pets to 'know' when their owners are on their way home.
2. The Sense of Direction – this ability accounts for the 'incredible journeys' some animals make to be with their owners, including homing pigeons.
3. Premonitions – which may explain why some animals seem to know when earthquakes and other events are about to occur.

1 Abstract from Sheldrake, R., Lawlor, C. and Turney, J., pp 57–74, 'Perceptive Pets: A Survey in London', *Biology Forum* 91, 1998)

1. TELEPATHY

In the section of Sheldrake's book on telepathy, he asserts that this ability arises from the strong bond that develops between humans and family pets. He relates several anecdotes from pet owners who believe that their animals are psychically picking up their intentions, and one story, about a mixed breed dog called Ginny, is particularly interesting. His owner told Sheldrake:

> *'I just cannot understand how my dog can know when I am going to walk him. Only my thinking of it is enough for him to jump about joyfully. In order to exclude the possibility of eye contact and information through the other senses, I left the dog outside in the garden and behind closed windows and doors when I thought of taking him. And still the same result every time: He acts crazy out of sheer joy and expectation. When I dress to leave for work, however, he remains totally quiet.'*

A friend of mine has a beautiful Springer Spaniel called Billy and he, too, has a wonderful knack of being able to distinguish between 'walkies' time and when John is simply opening the back door to go instead to the car, bike or simply out to the garden. At first we thought it could be argued that this very perceptive dog is picking up some kind of cues from John. Perhaps Billy was simply noticing his attire, or hearing him pick up the lead, or car keys, but as with Ginny, even if he decided on a quick walk through the fields in his work clothes, Billy was there, ready and waiting, while at other times when he went through the back door, he would remain on his bed without a flinch!

It has been argued that there could even be an odour cue which a human releases with a certain intention that only the dog can smell. More difficult to explain, however, is the story of a cat in Switzerland that seemed to know when a specific telephone call was coming:

> 'After my father had retired, he sometimes worked for an acquaintance in Aargau. Sometimes, he called us from there in the evening. One minute before this happened, the cat became restless and sat down next to the telephone. Sometimes, my father took the train to Biel and then used a moped to get home from there. Then the cat sat down outside the front door thirty minutes before he arrived. At other times, he arrived at Biel earlier than usual and then called us from the station, and the cat sat down near the telephone shortly before the call came. After it, she went to the front door. All this happened very irregularly, but the cat seemed to know exactly where he was and what would happen afterward.'

And, of course, there are anecdotes of dogs and cats who 'know' when their owners are coming home, such as that from T, who wrote:

> 'When I divorced my husband, I got an apartment alone with my cat, Bo. He always met me at the door when I came home from work, but that isn't the strange part.
> 'I decided to move across country and to save money I stayed with friends for two months before leaving. They told me that when it was time for me to come

home, Bo would sit in the front window and look for me, then run to check out the back door since I came in one way or the other. It's real odd because I never got off work at the same time every day – it always varied by two to five hours! But Bo always knew and waited for my return![2]

The actual word 'animal' derives from the Latin *anima*, which translates as life principle, breath, air, soul, or living being. Thus, recognition of the spiritual essence of animals and respecting them as fellow intelligent beings is vital. Some believe animals are able to communicate with humans who are open to the telepathic connection, comprehending their intentions, emotions, images, or thoughts behind the words, even if the words themselves aren't totally understood.

Perhaps this isn't such a weird concept when we consider that babies are born without any knowledge of language – babies pick up on the thoughts, intentions and body language of their parents and then language is learnt and becomes the main vehicle of communication. Yet speak to any body language expert and they will be quick to tell you the vast percentage of the language behind the words that comes from stance, stature and mannerisms. Does the same apply to the animal kingdom when it comes to comprehending humans? After all, we all know dog and cat body language – perhaps we are just as easy to read and our thoughts are the same?

Interestingly, and worthy of mention here is the story of Washoe the chimpanzee. She was born in Africa about forty

2 Taken from an account sent in for an article on
http://paranormal.about.com/library/weekly/aa021201b.htm

years ago and cross-fostered, that is removed from her biological parents and raised by surrogates. The special thing about Washoe is that she acquired American Sign Language from her human companions. Washoe is the first non-human animal to acquire a human language and her adopted son Loulis is the first to acquire a human language from another chimpanzee.

The four chimpanzees at the Chimpanzee and Human Communication Institute – Washoe, Loulis, Tatu and Dar – have all learnt extensive American Sign Language vocabularies and live together as a social group. They gesticulate and vocalise as free-living chimpanzees do, but also use American Sign Language in their interactions with humans and with each other to answer questions, make requests and describe activities and objects. This is phenomenal and really adds another dimension to the debate on animal telepathy and whether they know what we are thinking.[3]

I mentioned earlier the ability of some animals to 'know' when an earthquake is about to occur. Before the quake actually starts, rats and snakes have been seen fleeing their burrows, horses and other farm animals have become agitated and birds fly away from the scene in great flocks. Again, this is almost certainly a case of super-sensitivity to the environment rather than true precognition. The creative senses subtle vibrations, odours and electric and magnetic emissions resulting from the stresses within the earth.

3 For more details on this see http://www.friendsofwashoe.org/, http://www.geocities.com/RainForest/Vines/4451/TalkWithChimps.html, and http://deafness.about.com/cs/signfeats2/a/signinganimals.html

Much harder to explain, however, are incidents in which the pet truly seems to have foreknowledge of some disastrous event or problem – even knowing when friends, partners or colleagues are up to no good – an event for which there can be no sensory cues to pick up on. Sheldrake includes several interesting examples in his studies, including this one:

> One morning my dog, Toby, tried to stop me going out of the front door. He barged against me, leaned on the door, jumped up at me and pushed me. He is normally a quiet, loving dog and knows my routine; I would have been back within four hours. I had to lock him in the kitchen and left him howling, something he has never done before or since. I set off at 7.30 am and by 9.40 am I was involved in a horrific traffic accident resulting in a fractured neck and right arm, and many other injuries. In the future, I'll listen to Toby.'

When I was on a phone-in show for BBC Radio Newcastle, Joyce from Blythe called and recalled how her dog suddenly used to get up and go to the air-raid shelter minutes before the siren went off!

I also received some amusing anecdotes about animals knowing better than us about our choice of partners! One letter was from Jane Donovan about her perceptive cat Lulu, who liked to help her choose her partners! A few years ago, she was seeing a guy who Lulu made a point of showing her disgust and disapproval of him by sitting on his smart, black work trousers which deeply annoyed him. Later, when they were upstairs in bed, she snuck up behind him and sunk her claws into his bare backside. Suffice to say, not long afterwards their 'relationship' fizzled out, much to Lulu's delight!

Similarly, in Australia, pets were keen to let Susan Henderson know what they thought of her cheating husband. As she explains:

'I am, and always have been, an unashamed "cat woman". My estranged husband never has been; in fact, he openly says he hates cats. My cats have always slept on my bed and indeed slept with us for five years. However, at the time that it turned out he was having an affair, they shifted their sleeping positions to sleep around me, between us, and on his chest (which he hated with a passion)! As my husband's marital behaviour deteriorated (unbeknown to me at the time), the cats began to show their distaste and suddenly started to pee on his side of the bed (soaking his feet!), on the floor on his side of the bed (so that he put his foot in it as soon as he got up) and then on the kitchen floor where he would be the first to stand in the morning to make his cup of tea!

'Then they started peeing in his shoes. One even peed in the washbasket of his work clothes (no one else's) while I was hanging out the washing with the basket on the ground beside me. It got so bad that a cat-house was built outside for them to sleep in at night as we just couldn't understand their sudden bad behaviour. Well, then they started climbing in the window of his car and peeing on his car seat. When he wound up the windows, they peed on the roof and sprayed on his windscreen.

Every day. There were two other family cars, and they never peed on or sprayed either of those.... After he finally moved out, the cat living in his new home started peeing in his car. My cats still climb up onto his car and piddle down his windscreen whenever he turns up here, but since his departure the peeing in the house has come to an abrupt halt!'

All Susan's cats have been astute when it came to men... she recalls, 'When I was a teenager, my stepfather was a philandering husband too... thinking about it, our cat used to leave mutilated mice in his slippers!'

Sceptics write off all these occurrences, attributing this to the distinguishable sound of the car engine or the person's keys in the lock, or just the coincidence of knowing people or events would turn out the way they did. However, I can verify our daft childhood Basset hound always knew when Mum was on her way home – he would move from his bed at the back of the house to sit behind the front door about ten minutes before she pulled up in the drive, be it her arriving home from school at a regular time, or having popped out to the shops, or to visit friends. This is the case for so many pet owners.

2. THE SENSE OF DIRECTION

Long journeys to find their home and visits even to unfamiliar places by pets on their own are most intriguing, such as an American cat who once walked over 2,500 miles to find his carers after they had moved and left him behind by mistake! Sheldrake provides several examples in his book, including this remarkable tale:

'My father-in-law had a small farm and on it he kept a watchdog, Sultan. One day my father-in-law became ill and was taken to the hospital by ambulance. A few days later he died and then he was buried in the local graveyard, five kilometers from the farm. Several weeks after the burial the dog was not seen for days. This seemed strange to us, as Sultan never used to stray. But we did not make much of it, until one Sunday a former employee came along, who lived near the graveyard. She told us: 'Imagine, when I went across the graveyard the other day, Sultan lay at your family grave.' I cannot fathom how he could have found the way all these five kilometers. There were no footprints of his former master that he could follow. And he had never been taken to the graveyard, not even to the fields, since he had to keep watch at the house. How is it possible that he found his master's grave?'

This story links in well with one of old, that of Greyfriars Bobby in Scotland. John Gray, a gardener, together with his wife Jess and son John, arrived in Edinburgh around 1850. Unable to find work as a gardener, he avoided the workhouse by joining the Edinburgh Police Force as a night watchman. To keep him company through the long winter nights, John took on a partner, a diminutive Skye Terrier, his 'watchdog', called Bobby. Together John and Bobby became a familiar sight trudging through the old, cobbled streets of Edinburgh. Through thick and thin, winter and summer, they were faithful friends.

The years on the streets appear to have taken their toll on John, as he was treated by the police surgeon for tuberculosis.

He eventually died of the disease on 15 February 1858 and was buried in Greyfriars Kirkyard. Bobby soon touched the hearts of the local residents when he refused to leave his master's grave, even in the worst weather conditions. The gardener and keeper of Greyfriars tried on many occasions to evict him from the Kirkyard. In the end, he gave up and provided a shelter for Bobby by placing sacking beneath two tablestones at the side of John Gray's grave.

Bobby's fame spread throughout Edinburgh. It is reported that almost on a daily basis the crowds would gather at the entrance of the Kirkyard waiting for the one o'clock gun that would signal the appearance of Bobby leaving the grave for his midday meal. Bobby would follow William Dow, a local joiner and cabinet-maker to the same coffee house that he had frequented with his dead master, where he was given a meal. In 1867 a new bye-law was passed that required all dogs to be licensed in the city or they would be destroyed. Sir William Chambers (the Lord Provost of Edinburgh) decided to pay Bobby's licence and presented him with a collar with a brass inscription: 'Greyfriars Bobby from the Lord Provost 1867, licensed'. This can be seen at the Museum of Edinburgh. The kind folk of Edinburgh took good care of Bobby, but still he remained loyal to his master. For fourteen years, the dead man's faithful dog kept constant watch and guard over the grave until his own death in 1872.

Baroness Angelia Georgina Burdett-Coutts, President of the Ladies' Committee of the RSPCA, was so deeply moved by his story that she asked the City Council for permission to erect a granite fountain with a statue of Bobby placed on top. William Brody sculptured the statue from life, and it was unveiled

13

without ceremony in November 1873 opposite Greyfriars Kirkyard. And it is with that, that Scotland's capital city will always remember its most famous and faithful dog... [4]

Similarly, on the other side of the world, a dog named Hachiko went to a railroad Shibuya station in Tokyo, in Japan at 3.00 pm, to meet the train of his master, a Tokyo professor, and escort him home. When the professor died in the 1930s, Hachiko continued to visit the station every evening to greet the train, expecting to meet his master. For over nine years, the station staff and passengers used to notice the dog's loyal daily vigilance. No one was able to distract the dog. People there fed and cared for him until he died in 1935. Hachiko's admirers also raised money for a statue at Shibuya station in his memory. [5]

Shep belonged to a travelling sheep herder who was working in Montana, in America in the 1930s. In 1936, the shepherd died and Shep followed his master's coffin to the railway station at Fort Benton where it was being shipped back to his home town for burial. Shep was not allowed on the train, so from then on he hung around the station yard waiting for his master to come back. He waited and waited, checking every train that called at Fort Benton from 1936 through to 1942, when sadly Shep, now old, was himself killed by a passing train.

With renewed interest generated by the fiftieth anniversary of Shep's death, the community of Fort Benton organised a committee to produce a lasting memorial to their famous dog.

4 adapted from http://www.historic-uk.com/HistoryUK/Scotland-History/GreyfriarsBob.htm

5 http://lava.nationalgeographic.com/cgi-bin/aow/aow.cgi?day=24&month=1&year=02 and http://www.greyfriarsbobby.co.uk/hachiko.html

A beautiful site along the levee of the Missouri River was selected for the erection of an heroic-sized statue in bronze, sculptured by Bob Scriver. Known as Shepherd's Court, the site has quickly become the town's focal point.[6]

Another story which reiterates this phenomenon comes from John Owen, who phoned in to BBC Radio Newcastle when I was on talking about this book. His brother died suddenly aged just 24, in 1965. John recalled:

'Because there was a post mortem and an inquest, his body wasn't released for five days. When it eventually was, we had the coffin brought to the house for the evening and night before the funeral. Everyone was in the sitting room, but Mum had shut the family Labrador retriever outside, but he was scratching at the window wanting to come into the sitting room. We let him in and the dog sat in front of the coffin, sat up for about a minute, looked up and went away, as if paying his last respects. The funeral was arranged for the next morning and the family all attended and the next day, I walked with the dog to Jarrow Cemetery. I'd never been there with the dog before and once we reached the main gates, I let the dog off – it ran straight ahead and the grave was a good 100 yards ahead and he had to veer off to the right to the exact plot – a good 20 feet away and the dog went straight to the grave and sat there sniffing at the flowers and fresh soil – ignoring all the other new graves around it. By the time I caught up with him, he was sat on the grave – obviously smelling his master. Still, to this day, I think of that dog's phenomenal

6 http://www.greyfriarsbobby.co.uk/shep.html.

sense of smell – not only were we a distance from the grave but even then he was buried 5 feet down beneath the soil.'

There is also the well-documented case of an Italian dog, Fido, who waited close to twenty years for his owner's return. Every evening, Fido met his owner at the bus stop when he came home from work, but in 1943 his owner died in a bombing raid. However, Fido never gave up hope of seeing him again. Every evening for the next fifteen years, he returned to the bus stop to wait. *The Guinness Book of Pet Records* officially recognises Fido as the record holder for the longest canine vigil and the town rewarded his devotion with a memorial and gold medal.

There are also many stories about animals that have made long, sometimes arduous, journeys to be reunited with their owners, which are some of the most incredible and compelling cases for unexplained animal powers. There is the story of Ratty, the terrier, who takes himself on the bus on his own to the local pub. For a year, Ratty boarded the number 10 bus from his home, a farm in Dunnington, to travel to nearby York and meet up with old pals. The barmaid gave him sausages and no one minded Ratty, lame after a car ran over his foot, making the trip.

His owner Gary Kay tells the story: 'His travels started by accident. He must have happened to come across a bus and just got on. He got off when everyone else did – which was when it got to York – and walked straight into a pub. Folk fussed over him so much he started making a habit of it. On the first occasion, someone spotted my dog and phoned me.

But the barmaid lived in the next village, so she would bring him home in her car! He's a crackpot but everyone loves him!'

Ratty also hitches rides on the school bus with Gary's son, William, who is deeply impressed with his pet's antics: 'My mates think he's cool – he's my best pal.' As reported in the newspaper, the bus company First were quoted as saying, 'We don't charge dogs, so there's no reason why he can't get on!'[7]

One of Ann Irving's dogs went missing in the fog at her aunt's, some distance from her mum's house. 'It took him weeks,' she writes, 'but during all that time he was gradually working his way back home when someone spotted him from the newspaper story and pictures – so he didn't have to walk the whole distance!'

Candy is a five-year-old terrier-cross, who belongs to Mr Gale of Stoke Ferry, in Norfolk, and was nominated for the Friends for Life competition run by Crufts in 2006 after showing terrific bravery and courage when she went missing for five months. Being reunited with her owners was mainly down to the fact that she was registered with Petlog, the Kennel Club's pet reunification service. There are several versions of this service around, whereby a microchip is painlessly inserted under the skin, but when scanned brings up the owner's name and contact details and is something strongly recommended for all pet owners.

Candy went missing in March 2005 after escaping through a hole in the garden fence, leaving her owners devastated. They

7 Taken from 'New Landlord Bans the dog that takes a bus to his local pub' by Nick Fagge, p. 15, *Daily Express*, 31 July 2006

put up posters throughout the area, offering a reward for her return. Until October they heard nothing, when they received a call from Meadow Green Dog Rescue. It turned out that Candy had been brought in by the local council and they were able to identify her by scanning and reading her Petlog reference number on her microchip. Candy was in very poor condition with an injured front paw and a hole in her neck where someone had tried to remove the chip. She showed determination and bravery throughout her ordeal [8] and is now happily reunited with her family.

Mr Dudley, OBE, wrote about his family's collie-cross dog Josh, whom they obtained from a farm in Wales when he was nine months old. However, upon getting him home after the long drive from the farm they found that he was in fact a keen escapologist! Having their last dog, their garden was dog-proof, but Josh still got out. It then turned out that whenever he was off the lead he would run off, scramble or jump over the garden gate and fence until it got too much for his owners. The hard decision was made to take Josh to the nearest dog rescue centre. Once there, the Dudleys explained the situation, asking if they could take him in. As Mr Dudley wrote, 'During this conversation Josh sat quietly by my side, looking intently at the cages containing other dogs and at the warden. I was told they had no room but would have after a couple of days had elapsed…. Home we went, sad for Josh, my wife and myself.'

It's not so odd, but it is when you consider the fact that after they arrived home, Josh was a reformed creature, as Mr Dudley exclaimed, 'He never again as much as attempted to leave us!'

8 Crufts 2006, Friends for Life Competition, with permission

3. ANIMAL PREMONITIONS

Rupert Sheldrake explores the possibility that some animals can forewarn us of events that are about to occur. Most common, perhaps are pets that seem to know when their owners are about to have epileptic seizures. Explained in the simplest terms, epilepsy is a kind of temporary short circuit in the victim's brain, resulting in convulsions, laboured breathing and sometimes blackouts. Is it a real premonition the pet is having before the onset of such a seizure, or is the pet supersensitive to slight muscle tremors, subtle changes in behaviour, or emitted odours that even the victim is not aware of, minutes before the seizure takes hold? Sheldrake notes that pet dogs, cats and even rabbits can be sensitive to the event and this is something we explore further in Chapter 2.

He wonders whether animals are sensitive to other diseases as well and offers some anecdotal evidence that could suggest that some pets have warned diabetics when their blood-sugar was low and also stories of pets who seem to know the location of cancerous spots on their owners long before the diagnosis is made.

The following chapters will give anecdotes and explore instances in which animals have aided, and continue to aid us, in varying and diverse ways. How they do this, is for you, the reader, to determine.

CHAPTER 2

Natural Instinct

'If people were superior to animals, they'd take better care of the world.'

A. A. MILNE

All animals have keen senses that are based essentially on survival: to help them avoid predators, or to assist them in locating prey. It has been suggested that these senses might also help them detect pending disasters – as a part of their personal 'survival kit'. Many believe that animals can help man predict natural events, stating that animals act as messengers and partners to humans and there are countless stories documented of animals warning people of natural and physical disasters.

Dogs and cats are notorious for knowing when a tornado or earthquake are imminent and, of course, fish are reported to sink to the bottom of the ocean (and indeed fish tanks) prior to earthquakes. The behaviour of animals and their survival in the tsunami of 2004 has been well-documented. Such episodes demonstrate that, indeed, animals have a sixth sense or perception way beyond our own. Even more amazing is the fact that they consistently, compassionately and courageously use their awareness to aid humans – if only we would listen!

THE 2004 ASIAN TSUNAMI

After the tsunami, eyewitness accounts attested to the fact that animals offered better early detection cues than any man-made, technological systems. Despite the terrific human toll, few animals lost their lives – why?

Monkeys created an hiatus hours prior to the tsunami hitting, elephants broke free from their chains and made for higher ground. Such accounts made a positive aside to the horrendous grief and suffering which the tsunami brought, but perhaps we can delve more deeply beneath these news stories and suggest that this sixth sense is necessary and enhances the animal-human relationship. It is only at times like the tsunami that such bonds hit the headlines.

Peter Minns was sent over to Sri Lanka by ITV, and as he writes,

> 'Bodies were still being washed up on the coastlines of south and east Sri Lanka six months after the tsunami struck. I was there for ITV to see how much progress had been made in recovery – the answer was not much.
>
> 'Among the places I visited was Yala, a national park

which extended from the shores of the south coast. Yala was famous for its leopards, wild boar and elephants. Two hotels and a large bungalow catered for the thousands of visitors who came to see the animals.

'On the morning of the tsunami, the trackers who located the elephants for the guided tours noticed that they were behaving very strangely. The elephants began to climb the sand dunes. The first tour bus, a party of forty Japanese, followed the animals up onto the high ground. Had they stayed with them, they would have been safe, but they returned to their beach-side bungalow for breakfast. One hour later, the tsunami hit and all forty died.

'In Phuket, in Thailand, I was told of a young girl who was on an elephant ride. The animal suddenly broke away and carried the girl up into the jungle. The elephant handlers ran after it until it stopped on high ground. A short time later, the tsunami struck but the girl and the handlers were safe'.

Unlike the tragic human toll, no wild animal carcases were found along the coast of the Indian Ocean – in fact, wildlife officials at Sri Lanka's Yala National Park, where Peter had been – a wildlife reserve populated by hundreds of wild animals – reported no mass animal deaths. According to H. D. Ratnayake the deputy director of Sri Lanka's wildlife department, in a nearby Indian sanctuary containing 2,000 wildlife, only one (a boar) was killed by the tsunami. Putting it simply, in Sri Lanka, more than 30,000 people were killed when the tsunami struck, but all the elephants, deer and other wild animals survived.

EARTHQUAKES

George Pararas-Carayanni, a scientist who has been involved with tsunami research at the Institute of Geophysics of the University of Hawaii and a former director of UNESCO scientific organisations, says that since 1920, when an earthquake registering 8.5 hit China, the Chinese have been studying unusual animal behaviour. Before the 1966 earthquake in northern China, all the dogs in the village at the quake's epicentre ran from their kennels and survived.[1]

Author and animal disaster behaviour expert Diana L. Guerrero states that studies on this phenomenon go as far back as 373 BC in Italy, Greece, Chile and many other countries. In more modern times, one of the most compelling stories evolved when an earthquake measuring 7.3 on the Richter scale hit the city of Haicheng, in China, in 1975: In 1974, the Chinese were already observing animal behaviour – instances, among others, of snakes prematurely coming out of hibernation and rats suddenly appearing – to predict accurately the earthquake of 1975. Chinese and other scientists acknowledge that sharks, catfish and migrating birds sense electromagnetic changes in the earth. Two Chinese earthquakes have been predicted by paying attention to the accounts of people who reported unusual behaviour in cows, horses, mules, dogs, cats, goats and pigs.

By observing this strange animal behaviour before the earthquake, officials were able to alert the inhabitants and evacuate the city several days in advance. And it is not just

1 www.drgeorgepc.com/EarthquakePredictionChina.html

earthquakes: there are even stories of animals fleeing valleys in advance of avalanches and warning of German bomber squadrons approaching London during World War II.

Again, research conducted by Rupert Sheldrake and his colleague, David Jay Brown, has yielded accounts of dogs, cats, horses, emus, chickens, goats and caged birds becoming severely agitated prior to earthquakes in the San Fernando Valley, a suburb of Los Angeles. Sheldrake writes in *Dogs That Know When Their Owners Are Coming Home* (2000), 'Some people noticed that just before the earthquakes struck, there was a strange silence as wild birds and crickets stopped singing.'

He calls for an animal-based earthquake warning system with a toll-free hotline to receive calls about strange animal behaviour and reports that from 1979 to 1981, when the US Geological Service ran a pilot project[2] with 1,200 volunteer observers from earthquake-sensitive areas of California, the project found that seven of the earthquakes had a statistically significant increase in calls about unusual animal behaviour prior to their occurrence. Despite this, funding for the project was discontinued.

HOW DO ANIMALS DETECT EARTHQUAKES?

There are two theories as to how animals may be able to detect earthquakes. One is that they sense the earth's vibrations. Another, that they can detect changes in the air or gases released by the earth. There has been no conclusive evidence. It is a fact that Asian wild animals, like the animals at Yala National Park, were somehow able to detect the earthquake

2 For links, see http://biology.about.com/od/animalbehavior/a/aa123104a.htm

and move to higher ground before the tsunami hit, causing massive waves and flooding.

Other researchers are sceptical about using animals as earthquake and natural disaster detectors. They site the difficulty of developing a controlled study that can connect a specific animal behaviour with an earthquake occurrence. The United States Geological Survey (USGS) officially states:

> 'Changes in animal behavior cannot be used to predict earthquakes. Even though there have been documented cases of unusual animal behavior prior to earthquakes, a reproducible connection between a specific behavior and the occurrence of an earthquake has not been made. Because of their finely tuned senses, animals can often feel the earthquake at its earliest stages before the humans around it can. This feeds the myth that the animal knew the earthquake was coming. But animals also change their behavior for many reasons, and given that an earthquake can shake millions of people, it is likely that a few of their pets will, by chance, be acting strangely before an earthquake.'

It has been argued that elephants use their own type of infrasound technology, which detects movement deep within the earth, providing warnings of seismic activity that could save thousands of lives. Ironically, elephants were once thought to possess poor hearing. With such big ears, Nature would appear to have played a dirty trick indeed. But, in fact, elephants have advanced sound structures that enable them to communicate via infrasound over vast distances. And far from being the shy lumbering lumps they were once thought to be, it turns out that they are big talkers indeed.

Infrasound describes low-frequency sounds that fall below the range of human hearing. Elephants cannot only hear and, many researchers believe, feel, infrasound, but also emit it. In addition to the usual ta-run-ta-ra trumpeting and barking sounds audible to human ears, they have a second 'secret' language used for long distance 'phone' calls.

A perfect example of this is when, if you have been on safari, or even just watched a wildlife documentary, you have probably seen a herd of elephants suddenly stir from a watering hole, twitch their trunks, flap their ears and disperse without apparent warning. In fact, the warning was sounded – you just didn't hear it!

In ideal atmospheric conditions, elephants can communicate up to 9.8 km away and within a staggering 100-km² range. In the African evening, the air temperature within 300 m of the ground becomes inverted, causing low-frequency sound to be reflected back to the ground instead of dissipating into the sky as it normally does. In other words, elephants can talk over even greater distances after dark[3].

Thus, researchers believe that these wild animals were able to sense the danger long before humans – that via their sixth sense, or whatever you want to call it, they all knew it was coming. It's like birds who migrate to the same place year after year – a case of the higher and lower brain... we humans are fast losing this natural ability, perhaps it is something we can claw back through studying the animal kingdom who don't

3 Animals Did it First Critter Comm
http://www.animalplanet.co.uk/animalsdiditfirst/critter

have the materialism and stresses of the modern world to fill their heads with instead.

HURRICANES

Biologist Mike Heithaus explains the role of animal instinct in the Florida hurricanes that struck in 2004. In the twelve hours before Hurricane Charley hit Florida, fourteen electronically tagged sharks off Sarasota, who had never left their home region before, fled into deep waters and stayed away for two weeks before returning.

The same sharks reacted similarly when tropical storm Gabrielle was about to strike. Mike helps researchers understand the biology and behaviours of sea creatures from dolphins to sharks and turtles. [4]

MIGRATING BIRDS

An example of this 'sixth sense' is the simple, annual occurrence of birds migrating. Science regards the migratory habits of birds and other animals – species that have been following the same travel patterns for hundreds, even thousands of years – as 'instinctual behaviour' (what exactly is 'instinct', anyway?). Whatever this 'instinct', migration is one of the great mysteries of nature – no one is completely sure how they do it. Many birds migrate in large flocks, along

4 Tsunami: Animal Instinct Investigating Amazing Animal Instincts
http://www.animalplanet.co.uk/tsunamianimalinstinct/investigating/index.shtml

established routes, or *flyways*. Some, including hawks and vultures, swallows, swifts and nighthawks, fly during the day, perhaps using visual clues such as the angle of the setting sun (and the pattern of polarised light created), or land features, such as coastlines, mountains and rivers, and wind direction to guide them. Birds that travel by night or over vast ocean distances, such as warblers, swallows and thrushes, use a combination of star patterns, odour clues carried by prevailing winds and water, and possibly even the subtleties of the earth's magnetic field that these animals can 'feel'. At least some birds can detect ultraviolet radiations and very deep sound vibrations, such as distant ocean waves. When one set of cues is obscured, as the sun and stars may be by cloud cover, more reliance is placed on alternate cues. Putting it simply, though, we don't know nearly as much about bird migration as we would like.

PETS AND PREGNANT WOMEN

Although there is no scientific proof that pets sense their owners' pregnancies, there seem to be plenty of examples! Dogs and cats are able to detect differences in moods, posture, behaviour and body chemistry that could clue them in to the enormous change a pregnant woman is going through.

There are other signs your dog and cat will pick up on, too. They are masters at reading body language, so they will notice when your movements start to get more awkward. Pets are also highly attuned to changes in your daily routine – say, if you are not taking your dog for runs as often as you used to, if you are spending more time on the couch, or if family members are treating you with extra care.

It is common for dogs to go on alert and become overprotective of their expecting owner from the very beginning of her pregnancy. Trainers have reported working with dogs that growled, barked, or blocked doors with their bodies to prevent other family members – even the husband – from coming into the same room as the mum-to-be!

Because they are not as socially involved, theoretically, cats are less likely to go through these sorts of behavioural changes. However, most stories seem to imply the cat is protective of the unborn. One respondent wrote, 'When I was pregnant I used to go round to my friend's house, and her cats would go mad for it, lying all around the belly. Then my cat would also get snuggly on the belly, until my daughter started kicking him off from the inside!' This type of account is so common. Another woman, Mrs Betheridge, wrote how 'when I got pregnant my cat began to act less like a cat and more like a little baby! She used to lay on my belly all the time and even before I knew'.

Another lady talking of her daughter wrote, 'When she had just found out she was pregnant, her cat was always trying to sit on her tummy or right next to it… they definitely sensed it.' And some people's cats knew they were pregnant before they did, as Ellen Lawrence wrote: 'My cats somehow knew I was pregnant before I did! Every time I sat or laid down, they were there on my tummy! They had never ever done this before and I couldn't figure out what was going on until I took a pregnancy test! They remained this way for the entire nine months and then went back to their usual ways as soon as I'd given birth!'

Sadly, though, some seem to interpret it with jealousy and may feel neglected. Cats can become more aggressive or act up by urinating where they are not supposed to, like in your bed, or laundry basket, as Miranda Green wrote, 'We just had to get rid of our cat because he could sense I was pregnant. For the past four months, since I conceived he has changed completely and took to scratching me anytime he was near my belly… he just hated it for some reason! He'd bite me, scratch me… but only my belly! He could obviously sense it and didn't want another baby in the house to steal his limelight!'

So, although scientists disagree as to whether animal behaviour can be used to predict natural disasters, they all agree that it is possible for animals to sense changes in the environment before humans. Researchers around the world continue to study animal behaviour and disasters, especially earthquakes. We can only hope in the not too distant future – if the findings are conclusive – that these studies will help to aid earthquake predictions and save human lives[5].

There seems no question that animals and their attempts to alert people to danger would add valuable information to sophisticated scientific systems. Instead of scoffing at the belief that animals have a sixth sense, or concluding that people who try to observe and understand animal communications are off-base, maybe it is time to take a look at all we humans might be missing. Instead of viewing animals as property, dumb beasts, or naïve and helpless children, let's give them the respect they are due. Animals don't speak our language, yet when humans

5 US Department of the Interior, US Geological Survey-Earthquake Hazards Program: URL: http://earthquake.usgs.gov

start listening for and watching their instinctive cues, the reduction of suffering and destruction will have powerful allies.

Since they have lived on earth longer than humans, perhaps they are genetically designed to know or sense more than humans? Have we lost innate abilities that used to warn and protect us? Would human lives be saved if people paid more attention to the sentient beings in their homes or gardens, in the countryside, and in nature?

CHAPTER 3

Animals and Superstition

'There is an Indian legend which says when a human dies there is a bridge they must cross to enter into heaven. At the head of that bridge waits every animal that human encountered during their lifetime. The animals, based upon what they know of this person, decide which humans may cross the bridge... and which are turned away...'

ANON

Following on from the last chapter and seeing the role that cues from animals could play in our daily life, let's explore avenues in which animals have been, and still are, utilised in ways no man-made machine could be.

In medieval times, a howling dog was considered to be an omen of misfortune or death. If a dog howled when a baby was born, it signified that that child would have an unhappy life, or be susceptible to the darker side of its nature. Howling outside a house would cause great concern to the occupants, as this again was considered to be an ill omen. In Ireland, a rural belief is that if a strange dog digs up someone's garden it foretells illness or death; while in America, a dog that sleeps with its tail out straight behind it and with paws upturned is an indication that bad news is coming. The direction the tail is pointing, it is said, shows the direction from which the bad news will come.

While many stories represent bad omens, so too is there a plentiful number suggesting the dog and its behaviour are linked to good fortune. Beliefs, such as if a dog runs under a table, then a thunderstorm is on the way go back through history. Some say that if a strange dog follows you, this is a sign of good luck. If a black-and-white dog should cross someone's path, this indicates the business in which that person is engaged will have a good outcome. (It is interesting that cats also have been endowed with the ability to herald good or bad luck in different circumstances and colours to the dog.)

The name of a famous cure for a hangover, 'the hair of the dog', developed from an activity in medieval times and was supposed to be a cure for a bite from a mad dog. The belief was that if the person who was bitten by a mad dog ate some of that dog's hairs with a slice of bread and some rosemary, they would be protected. Another version was to bind the wound with some hairs from the dog and some herbs to gain the protection.

ANIMALS AS WEATHER FORECASTERS

Can animals help predict the weather? Many claim dogs act up before thunderstorms, tornados and other inclement weather due to their keen ability to detect fluctuations in barometric pressure, which produces the dog's anxiety and behaviour. This evolutionary behaviour can be traced back to wolves, who used it to know when to move the pack to shelter before big storms. There are folkloric traditions suggesting that animals act on their instincts and can accurately predict weather changes – and in some cases, scientists can back this up...

For centuries, shepherds and sailors – people whose lives and livelihoods depend on the weather – relied on lore to foretell tomorrow's weather. They showed a keen sense of observation and quickly connected changes in nature with rhythms or patterns of weather.

Farmers watched cloud movement and the sky colour to know when to sow and reap. Mariners noted wind shifts and watched wave motions for signs of change. Hunters studied the behaviour of insects and animals and, through repeated observation, learned to foretell the weather. They recalled what they saw in the form of short sayings, often embodied in rhyme for ease of memory. The beliefs of thousands of people were passed down from generation to generation, altered by the wisdom of the times. They became part of culture and education, and came to the New World and different climates with the waves of migration.

Many weather proverbs are nothing more than familiar rhymes, light-hearted ditties or imaginative contradictions. Some have survived the test of careful observation and scientific reasoning to become reliable guides to forthcoming change in the weather. Only those sayings that prophesy daily change, usually pertaining to sky appearance, cloud movement or wind change, have any hope of success. Lore involving key dates or anniversaries, or suggesting monthly or seasonal change, can only be right by chance.

For centuries, people have been forecasting the weather. Although things now are more scientific, those before us who looked to plants and animals for hints about what the weather would do were not entirely wrong. For example, before it rained, some people often observed that ants moved to higher ground, cows lay down, pine cones opened up, frogs croaked more frequently and sheep's wool uncurled. Birds also roost early and feed heavily before a rain shower or snow, and pigs and squirrels gather more debris to insulate themselves from cold weather. Over the years, people began to notice other natural clues to upcoming weather, and several weather 'sayings' grew up over the years.

When looking at weather proverbs, though, we do need to keep this in mind: they are usually based on someone's observations and not on scientific studies. Because climates and weather patterns differ throughout the world, a weather proverb based on observations in one location may not be valid in another. Some proverbs arose simply from coincidence, not weather patterns, and therefore may seldom hold true. But under some circumstances, certain proverbs do hold up to science. Here are some that, under the right circumstances, have proven valid:

CATS – 'IF CATS LICK THEMSELVES, FAIR WEATHER.'

During fair weather, when the relative humidity is low, electrostatic charges (static electricity) can build up on a cat as it touches other objects. Cat hair loses electrons easily, so cats become positively charged. When a cat licks itself, the moisture makes its fur more conductive so the charge can 'leak' off the cat. In fair weather, during high pressure, dry air sinks from above. Relative humidity is low and cat hair becomes a better insulator. Many cats don't like to be petted during cold winter weather when the humidity is low because sufficient charge builds up to cause small sparks which irritate them (and the person petting them).

CRICKETS

Crickets are accurate thermometers; they chirp faster when warm and more slowly when cold. They are extremely accurate. Count their chirps for fourteen seconds, then add forty and you have the temperature (in fahrenheit) of wherever the cricket is.

FLIES – FLIES BITE MORE BEFORE A RAIN

This rule does not always apply, but insects do call more during moist weather, as flying is harder. Heat causes human sweating, which makes for a more appetising target. These two reasons, plus a release of more body odours when atmospheric pressure on your body lowers, add up to the rule that flies and insects are more bothersome just before a rain than at any other time.

COWS – A COW WITH ITS TAIL TO THE WEST, MAKES WEATHER THE BEST; A COW WITH ITS TAIL TO THE EAST, MAKES WEATHER THE LEAST.

This New England saying has much truth in it, for an animal grazes with its tail to the wind. This is a natural instinct, so the animal may face and see an invader, while the scent of an invader from the opposite side would carry to the cow in the wind. In as much as an east wind is a rain wind and a west wind is a fair wind, the grazing animal's tail becomes a weather sign.

SEA GULLS – 'SEA GULL, SEA GULL, SIT ON THE SAND; IT'S A SIGN OF A RAIN WHEN YOU ARE AT HAND'[1]

Generally speaking, birds will roost more during low pressure than high-pressure. Before a hurricane a great flock of birds will be seen roosting. Perhaps the lowering of pressure or thinning of air density makes flying so much harder; the lessening of natural updrafts would also account for the birds 'resting it out'.

Here are some more well-known sayings:

When you see a beaver carrying sticks in its mouth,
It will be a hard winter, you'd better go south.

Expect the weather to be fair,
When crows fly in a pair.

When chickens scratch together,
There's sure to be foul weather.

Flies bite more before a storm.

1 Compiled by Vera Schlanger, Hungarian Meteorological Service, Scientific reviewing: Dr Ildikó Dobi Wantuch/Dr Elena Kalmár, Hungarian Meteorological Service, Budapest; http://www.atmosphere.mpg.de/enid/5057ce0c8397e666f5a77ee2a0017790,55a304092d09/1qx.html

When ladybugs [ladybirds] swarm,
Expect a day that's warm.

The hooting of an owl,
Says the weather will be foul.

If the rooster crows at night,
He's trying to say rain's in sight.

While animal behaviour is varied and fascinating, but it is sometimes very difficult to understand why animals behave in the way that they do. Because of this, a number of myths have grown up around them. For instance, it is believed that the ostrich buries its head in the sand when faced with danger, hence the expression. However, this is not true (when an ostrich sits on its nest, its reaction to danger is to lower its head towards the ground. The ostrich hopes its enemy will then mistake it for a termite mound or low bush!).

BEES

'If bees stay at home,
Rain will soon come.
If they fly away,
Fine will be the day'

Australians have used the apiarist whose bees accurately predicted heavy falls one December to predict rainfall. Keith Brooke's bees were closing off entrances to the hives and showing other similar behaviour to that of 1988, a year of extreme rains. Brooke said it was likely there would be a few major falls in the region during the summer months. After a wet December, with good rains across the region, Keith Brooke said that while overall gauges might be less than originally expected, the bees were indicating that rain was definitely on the way... And he was right![2]

2 Bees predict more rain: http://www.abc.net.au/rural/nt/stories/s467774.htm

CHAPTER 4

Dogs as Working Partners

'The greatness of a nation and its moral progress can be judged by the way its animals are treated.'

GANDHI

This chapter and the next consist of the real specialists in their field, who excel in their line of work. Over the centuries, dogs have been selectively bred to become working dogs, including service dogs, guard dogs, hunting dogs and farm herding dogs. Dogs are also used to search for and rescue people and animals, such as in avalanches, at disaster sites and to find missing people or pets. In Chapter 5, you will read about registered assistance dogs who are specially trained to help their disabled human owners and how their support often works better than that of a human carer. The majority of modern working dogs are put in positions which capitalise on the advantages of their sensory abilities or their strength and endurance, which are better than those of humans and are thus irreplaceable.

Arguably, the working group consists of some of the most heroic canines in the world, who aid humans in many walks of life, and include the Boxer, Great Dane and St Bernard and the Labrador-retrievers and German Shepherds who are more common among the police and, of course, Collies who are more at home on working farms.

SEARCH AND RESCUE DOGS

Dogs who rescue humans are no new phenomenon. In the seventeenth century, monks initially used dogs to help travellers negotiate the Great St Bernard Pass. It was soon realised that the dogs could also find people buried in snow by scent. In World War I, the Red Cross used dogs to find injured men on the battlefields. A search for the survivors of an avalanche in Switzerland sowed the seed of an idea, which led to dogs being trained just for search work and later led to the establishment of the Swiss Alpine Club and the development of rescue networks in other countries.

Dogs instinctively know how to find things and how to retrieve. The handler and dog work together as a team and the dog is at its happiest doing what its instincts tell him to do. Dogs can be trained to find very specific things in all kinds of places, such as up a tree, in the woods or a field, in a handbag or suitcase, in a car, on a street, in a closet, under rubble or collapsed buildings, or in deep water or under snow. There is a close connection between Search and Rescue Animals (SAR), their handlers and government bodies, as the dogs are sometimes scrambled to trail escaped convicts or suspects from crime scenes.

Humans shed dead skin cells, which give off gasses and vapours and these all act as a unique scent, which a dog can use as a 'fingerprint' for each person. Dogs' sense of smell has been estimated to be at least a million times more refined than ours, with as many as 220 million olfactory nerve endings, compared to a human's mere 5 million. They can also detect sound vibrations at 250 yards, which most humans can barely hear at 25 and, most importantly, these marvellous workers are dedicated, determined and motivated beyond the limits of exhaustion, as no human or machine could ever be,[1] picking up a scent and following it, sometimes from as far as half a mile away, depending on the conditions.[2]

Rescue dogs are trained specifically to detect traces of sweat and other musky odours exuded by the body during stress. They are also able to distinguish between the living and the dead.

TRACKING, TRAILING AND AREA SEARCH DOGS

Dogs are used to find people by following their trail. There are two main ways of doing this, although they're really at two ends of the a continuum. Tracking is the process in which the dogs follows the person's exact path and trailing is where the

1 Statistics taken from http://dogsinthenews.com/issues/0110/articles/011006a.htm

2 http://www.fbi.gov/kids/dogs/know.htm

dog follows the person's scent, which may or may not approximate the path the person took, due to factors affecting the dispersal of scent such as wind and temperature. Contrary to popular opinion, water does not disrupt a tracking or trailing dog. If the water has carried surface scent away, the dog will simply cast around for the trail on the other side (if the water is still, the scent remains on the surface of the water). Dogs can even trail people in cars from the scent that blows out of the window, or through the vents of the car!

Quite often no scent article is available and in case such as this dogs trained in area search can be employed instead. These dogs air scent (that is, test the air rather than follow a specific scent) and search for any human scent. This is most often used in wilderness searches to find anyone hiding in a building or other confined areas.

DISASTER SEARCH

Some SAR dogs are trained to search through rubble for survivors of earthquakes or landslides. In this scenario, the dog is not looking for a specific person, as is the case with tracking and trailing. Instead, the dog is looking for any human scent. Avalanches, collapsed buildings, aeroplane and train crashes are all examples where this kind of dog is employed.

CADAVER SEARCH

As well as alive or injured people, dogs are also trained to find corpses, new or old. Some dogs are employed on archaeological digs to help locate old graves whereas others are used by the police to find the bodies of people who have only recently died, or to collect all the bones found in an area. Others find drowning victims in water. This is a rapidly expanding field, with new methods of training currently being developed worldwide.

NARCOTICS AND EVIDENCE DOGS

This area is commonly considered a subset of SAR. Dogs can be trained to alert (by barking, pointing or pawing) their handlers to the presence of controlled substances such as drugs, agricultural products (at customs and borders), and nearly anything else, from gunpowder (to detect guns), bomb and arson materials to foodstuffs, even money. Narcotic dogs are trained to search through buildings, cars and luggage for a scent that will assist in the apprehension of a smuggler. They can be trained to alert more than one kind of drug, and can do so despite ingenious efforts on the smugglers' part, with dogs known to have located drugs concealed in petrol, rotting food and skunk oil. They can be trained to discriminate between large and small amounts. In fact, some dogs are trained to whiff passing vehicles; if one is detected as suspicious it can be stopped and searched later without directly involving the dog and its handler.

Evidence dogs are trained to search for items bearing human scent, sometimes that of a specific human. They are utilised in crime scenes to find evidence thrown away by a suspect. If handled properly, such as evidence can later be used by a

Bloodhound to link the scent left on it to a suspect, with several cases deemed admissible evidence in court.

In 1963, Hamish MacInnes, the leader of the Glencoe Mountain Rescue Team, had become interested in using dogs for search and rescue. He was invited by the International Red Cross to attend a conference in Switzerland about training dogs for search and rescue, and after the trip he was convinced that search dogs were a great asset to all rescue teams. This resulted in the Search and Rescue Dog Association (SARDA) being born.

The exceptional courage of the dogs and handlers of SARDA work with the Mountain Rescue Teams (MRTs) in the most inhospitable areas of the Pennines, in Wales and in Scotland, bringing injured and lost individuals down from places of certain death if they are not found in time. All too often a search does not have a happy ending, be it a fatality on the mountain, or an injured handler or dog.

SARDA England's search dogs are trained to 'air scent', meaning they do not, as a general rule track, the missing person. The dogs will react to a human scent being blown towards them by the wind or air currents. So as long as the dog is searching downwind of a casualty, or items that have human scent on them, they should find them.

In bad conditions, a dog can cover large areas of ground in the search for a missing person. The dog is very sensitive to any human scent it finds and will immediately follow that scent to where a human is located. It will then indicate to its handler to let them know it has had a 'find'. It matters not whether it is dark or visibility is very poor, the dog can search just as well as if it were a clear day.

If there is no wind or it is storm force, the human scent will not carry as far before it is recognised by the dog. The handler has to compensate for this by shortening his or her sweeps of the area, so it takes more time to search to get a high probability of detection.[3]

Sam, a golden Labrador, was at first considered by his breeder to have lots of faults. She was used to breeding for the show ring and he was not up to the standard. John and Tina, a couple who were soon to move home to Cumbria, bought him and the adventure began.

Once settled in Cumbria, they were told stories about the SARDA dogs. Fascinated to begin with, they took Sam off to basic training lessons, but he got bored. After taking some advice from a friend, John approached the SARDA group in his area and he and Sam were put through their paces. Training is strict and tough. The team cannot have a dog or handler that is not up to scratch; they would be a liability.

After a doubtful start as a young dog with a mind of his own, Sam passed his training schedule and went on to become one of the greatest search and rescue dogs of the country. He and John have saved more than a few souls. The price of fame is never cheap, with it comes the injuries and exhaustion that all dogs and handlers have to endure. Sam nearly died when he plunged 40 feet over the edge of a crag while working. John clambered down the steep gorge and then, with Sam unconscious in his arms, he ran back to the team waiting to save him.

Sam received many honours while he was an active search

3 Taken with permission from http://www.sardaengland.org.uk/whydogs.htm.

dog. He was a devoted family member when off-duty, always loving and sweet natured to the couple's two children. When his duties were reduced as he got older, he helped bring on younger dogs. However, he was still on active duty and showing the younger search dogs how it should be done when he was nine years old[4].

Another search and rescue dog received a rare award for saving the life of a depressed man after he went missing from home. Meg, a five-year-old Border Collie, and her handler, Des Toward, were the stars of a ceremony at Sandown Park Racecourse, near London, where they were awarded a gold medal by the Pro Dogs Group.

The pair, who are members of the Teesdale and Weardale Search and Rescue Team, have been involved with a number of life-saving rescues in the north east. Their fourth successful rescue mission in a year came to the attention of Pro Dogs, which highlights the bravery and efforts of dogs around the country, when Meg was nominated by Chief Inspector Dave Carroll of Durham Police.

In December 1999, Meg and Des, from the Teesdale village of Cotherstone, found a 51-year-old man, who was suffering from depression and had gone missing from his home in Crook. Within twenty minutes of starting the search, in woodland, near Brancepeth, in County Durham, Meg had picked up his trail and soon after discovered the man, who was suffering from hypothermia. Des Toward, 37, said, 'If Meg hadn't found him when she did, the man would have died. There are several other people who we have found in the nick of time. She really is a remarkable dog.'

4 Read Sam's story in *Search Dog* by Angela Locke, Souvenir Press, London, 1989

Last year, Meg also found a lost walker in Osmotherley, and then sniffed out an elderly woman, who was discovered hiding under a bush, after disappearing from her Newton Aycliffe home. Her third rescue came in October, when she found an elderly man from Kirkbymoorside, near Scarborough, who was wandering in an isolated area at 3am.[5].

Another story is that of a pet dog who assisted a search-and-rescue team to pinpoint his and his owner's whereabouts. Pensioner Mark Corrie collapsed in a remote wood while walking Boz, his daughter's black Labrador dog. For two days and two nights the seventy-four-year-old lay helpless on the wooded hillside in Cumbria, with nothing to eat or drink. But thanks to Boz's courage and unflinching loyalty, Mr Corrie survived his ordeal. The superdog stayed by the pensioner's side, repeatedly barking for help.

He was still there and continued barking forty-eight hours after Mr Corrie's worried wife raised the alarm when he did not return home for lunch. Police officers, members of ten mountain-rescue teams and an RAF helicopter became involved in the weekend search operation. The next day, ninety-seven people, including many local residents, volunteered to help scour the countryside. Finally, search teams looking for the missing walker heard Boz's barking and the dog effectively guided them to the stricken great-grandfather.

Mr Corrie, who was rescued on his seventy-fourth birthday, was dehydrated from two days without food or water but otherwise unhurt. He was found in a confused state and taken

5 http://www.theclarion.co.uk/the_north_east/petscorner/features/meg.html A golden day for rescue hero Meg, 6 December 2000

off the fell by stretcher before being airlifted to Cumberland Infirmary in Carlisle[6].

Society owes trained SARDA dogs, such as Sam and Meg, as well as loyal and faithful pets like Boz, a debt of gratitude. Without these dogs and handlers there would be many more fatalities in the inhospitable areas on the moors and mountains that are enjoyed by so many who walk and pursue leisure activities.

UK FIRE SERVICE – URBAN SEARCH AND RESCUE DOG TEAM

This team was officially formed in July 2001 to give the UK Fire Service a search-and-rescue dog team capability to respond to UK USAR and international incidents. The teams are made up of firefighters from individual brigades throughout the country, who are on standby 365 days a year for immediate deployment. Teams have the full logistical support of the UK Fire Service for UK operations and, for overseas disasters, that of the Department for International Development (DIFD).

The primary role USAR is to assist emergency services in the United Kingdom and overseas.

ASIAN TSUNAMI

The following report is a brief overview of the experiences of Sub Officer Hampton and Divisional Officer Andy Dermott,

6 'Hero Labrador alerts rescuers to sick owner', *Daily Mail*, Chris Brooke, 22.00 p.m., 15 August 2006;
http://www.dailymail.co.uk/pages/live/articles/news/news.html?in_article_id=400754&in_page_id=1770&in_a_source

who are both members of the Leicestershire Fire and Rescue UKFSSART team and who were deployed to Thailand in response to the Boxing Day tsunami.

'Our assistance was requested on Boxing Day, and we flew out to Thailand on 27 December and returned on 1 January.

'Following our arrival in Bangkok, we transferred to a flight for Phuket and once there, travelled north to the town of Takua Pa in Phang Nga province. This was the principal town in the province and was the command centre for the provincial Local Emergency Management Authority.

'We met up with the Search Dog Unit and were informed that we would be working in the Khoa Lak area. The following morning (Wednesday, 29 December) we travelled to the area of operations. The major in command of the team decided to split the team in two, with both me and Keith acting as an advisor to a sub section of three dogs, their handlers, body recovery teams and a section commander. One team was tasked with continuing search operations in the Sofitel Magic Lagoon, Khoa Lak, where the day before the team had recovered approximately 100 bodies. That morning other military units, a German team and ourselves located and recovered another forty bodies. In the afternoon, we rejoined the other team, who had earlier been searching a construction site on the Khoa Lak peninsular. These searches had located nearly 150 bodies although over 100 were not recovered at that time as they were in a basement.

'A joint search was then carried out on a hotel complex that was largely used by Scandinavians. This hotel was also located on the Khoa Lak peninsular. The search revealed only a few bodies. During the search we met a Norwegian police officer who informed us that there were nearly 1,200 Scandinavians (the majority of whom were Swedes) missing.

'The next day (30 December) the team returned to the Khoa Lak peninsular area and this time we were tasked with completing a search of a hotel complex called the Bamboo Orchard, where there were 70 persons still unaccounted for. The team again split into two and searched different parts of the complex. Again, only bodies were recovered. This search took most of the day.

'At the end of this search, the major in command withdrew the team back to our base at Takua Pa. Once there, he liaised with the military command team and, as a result, the team was stood down as it was rightly decided that there was now little chance of locating any live survivors.

'Keith and I left Takua Pa on the evening of the 30th, stayed that night in Pkuket and then caught an early morning flight to Bangkok. At Bangkok, we were able to book seats on that evening's flight to London, where we arrived at 06.30 the following day.[7]

BOSCASTLE, CORNWALL FLOODS

During the summer of 2004, two rescue dogs from the Mid-West Wales Fire and Rescue Service were handed their first

7 http://www.ukfssartdogteams.org.uk/tsunami.htm

mission – to help find victims of flash flooding, which caused devastation in Cornwall. Fflam, a Border Collie and Sam, a springer spaniel, were flown by helicopter to join the search at Boscastle in the north of the county. They formed part of a team of ten fire service rescue dogs on duty. Following flash flooding and torrential rain, up to fifteen people were still unaccounted for.

Sam, who was based in Carmarthen, and Fflam, from Pontardawe, boarded an RAF air sea rescue helicopter at 9.30am. on Tuesday 17 August, the day after the entire month's rainfall fell in just two hours. The Mid and West Wales Fire and Rescue Service was asked for assistance just hours earlier. A spokeswoman for the service said at the time, 'This is Sam and Fflam's first official job, although they were put on alert following an explosion in Glasgow earlier this year. The dogs have been accompanied by their handlers, Arwel Hughes, from Cross Hands, who looks after Flam, and Alex Baum, from Carmarthen, who looks after Sam.' The town was littered with upturned trees and crumbling walls, which hampered the efforts of police divers and a body recovery team who worked alongside the rescue dogs before the clean-up operation got underway[8].

BIRMINGHAM TORNADO

Two USAR dog teams responded to assist the West Midlands Fire and Rescue Service USAR team in the aftermath of the Birmingham tornado disaster. On the afternoon of Thursday 28 July, the City of Birmingham was hit by a tornado which caused extensive damage to buildings, resulting in the West

8 http://www.ukfssartdogteams.org.uk/boscastle.htm.

Midlands Fire and Rescue Service (WMFRS) declaring a major incident. The Sparkbrook, Balsall Heath, Moseley and Kings Heath areas were worst hit, and West Midlands Ambulance Service confirmed that it treated twenty patients, including three with serious injuries.

Peterborough in Cambridgeshire was also hit in the late afternoon. Police said the high winds caused structural damage in the Paston area of the city but they were not aware of anyone being hurt. At around six o'clock in the evening, a request was made for assistance from the UK Fire Service Dog Team. Their website reports that a team was in attendance by 6:50pm and was immediately deployed to search for persons reported in collapsed structures in the Ladypool Road area. They cleared six buildings in various states of collapse, where the occupiers had not been seen since the tornado had struck. This took a considerable amount of time as the buildings were in a dangerous state and littered with broken glass and other sharp objects, which presented a real hazard to Jake, one of the search and rescue dogs. Finally, they cleared a garage where the roof had collapsed over the cars on the forecourt.

Thankfully, no one was trapped. To keep Jake's spirits up, one of the WMFRS USAR team was hidden so that he could make a live find. Jake and his handler were soon joined by Arwel Hughes, Roger Howells and his dog Flamm from Mid and West Wales Fire and Rescue Service at around 21.30 hours. Soon afterwards, the incident commander took the decision to withdraw the Fire Service and to stand by throughout the night.

The search and rescue dogs then redeployed to Highgate Fire Station, where they caught up on some well-earned rest.

The decision was taken at the Silver Command briefing on the morning of 29 July to withdraw the Fire Service on the basis that all persons were accounted for. Following this, the respective dog teams returned home, having impressed the WMFRS personnel with their professionalism and work rate.

POLICE DOGS

Dogs play a vital role in modern police work and all police forces in the UK have a dog unit. The most popular breed for police work is the German Shepherd. Chosen for their intelligence and highly developed senses, they also tend to be more instinctively suspicious of strangers than other breeds. Dogs need to have the right temperament to be suitable for police work – those who may make unsuitable pets, because they are too energetic and demanding, are often ideal. There are approximately 2,500 police dogs in England and Wales, who aid police in finding drugs, explosives and human remains. Police dogs are also trained to track and catch criminals, for crowd work and to work in prisons.

A police dog must have a close bond with their handler for them to work successfully together. To create this bond, the dogs are matched with their handlers while they are still puppies and go to live with them when they're around 12 weeks old. However, they are very much working dogs, not family pets, so they live in kennels outside their handler's home. They begin their formal training together when the dogs are a year old.

Just as the dogs are carefully chosen, so are the police

officers with whom they will be working. Officers who volunteer to become dog handlers must have already completed two years of street duty as a uniformed Police Constable. Once approved the prospective handler attends a two-week suitability course. The police dog training course has been developed to prepare them for any situation they may face and builds on their instinctive behaviour to enable them to carry out tasks and obey the handler on command. A dog's natural instinct is to please their pack leader, and for a police dog this is their handler.

The course starts with basic obedience exercises. This is followed by tracking, where the dogs learn to follow a ground scent over different types of terrain and in varying conditions. They are taught how to bark continuously when they find what they are looking for. Not only that, they also learn how to chase and attack, even when they are being threatened with weapons. Police dogs need to be aggressive, but never vicious and they have to obey their handlers at all times. At the end of 14 weeks, the dogs should be ready to go out to work with their handler, with whom they will continue working until they are seven or eight years old.

Out on patrol, police dogs are used for searching and tracking situations. A police dog is able to search an area much more quickly than a lone officer, as well as being able to get into difficult places, such as dense undergrowth. The dog's ability to scent humans is also very useful in finding people who may be lost or hiding.

Dogs are also used in areas where there are large crowds – for example, at football matches, or other places where there may be incidents of anti-social behaviour. Specialist dogs are trained to search for drugs, explosives and fire-arms. For this work, Springer Spaniels and Labradors are often used because of the breeds' natural tracking abilities. As the threat of terrorism has increased these specialist police dogs have become even more important.

Piracy fighters at the Federation Against Copyright Theft (FACT) have recently trained a pair of dogs to locate DVDs. As part of a project promoted by the Motion Picture Association of America, FACT instigated the training of two black Labradors named Lucky and Flo. After eight months, the canines could identify DVDs among other items of cargo.

Lucky and Flo were put to put to the test at FedEx's UK hub at Stansted Airport, where they were successful in identifying packages and parcels containing DVDs. Customs officers who opened these packages discovered that all were legitimate shipments. Sniffer dogs can usually be trained only to detect one illicit item, normally either explosive substances or drugs. You might be forgiven for thinking that the effort spent in teaching Lucky and Flo to detect DVDs would have been better spent elsewhere, especially when you consider that fake DVDs smell no different from legitimate items. Despite the dogs' failure to find any stolen goods, FACT proclaimed the initiative a success.

'This is the first time dogs have been used anywhere in the world to search for counterfeit DVDs and the results were amazing,' said FACT director general Raymond Leinster. 'With the cooperation and assistance of FedEx and Customs, we were able to properly test the dogs in a real-life situation and prove that they can work in a busy airport environment.'

Mary Callahan, director of optical disc operations, worldwide anti-piracy at the MPAA, added, 'Lucky and Flo's immediate success in locating DVDs in transit offers us a new and highly effective means of detection for counterfeit discs'.[9]

Most dogs have such highly developed scenting abilities that they can recognise smells so diluted that even the most advanced of scientific instruments cannot measure them. Take Sauer, a Doberman trained by Detective Sergeant Herbert Kruger, for example. In 1925, without helicopters and thermal imaging equipment, he tracked a stock thief 100 miles across the Great Karrooin in South Africa – an area in excess of $400,000km^2$ used mainly for farming – by scent alone!

Similarly, between 1946 and 1961, Dox worked with his master, a police officer in Italy. The German Shepherd could follow a scent for 12 miles (19 kilometres). As a result of his work, the police captured 563 criminals. The dog also found 136 missing persons. His abilities earned Dox eleven gold medals and twenty-seven silver ones.[10]

And we're not just talking dogs either. In central Russia, Rusik the cat is the latest weapon in the battle against fish thieves. A year ago, he walked into the police station as a stray kitten, but now he helps police by sniffing out illegal cargoes of fish.

The fish that Rusik sniffs out are sturgeon and these are killed by fishermen, who sell their eggs as expensive 'caviar'. But sturgeon are facing extinction and it is illegal to catch them, so Rusik is on the case. The police say that no matter

9 Copyright police train sniffers to find DVDs;
http://www.theregister.co.uk/2006/05/11/gogs_hunt_dvds/
10 *National Geographic online;*

how well the smugglers hide the fish, Rusik is always able to point his nose in the right direction and find them.[11]

FARM AND SPORTING DOGS

A chapter on dogs working with man must include the dogs that attend to our countries' farms or, indeed, retrievers who work on drives in the season retrieving pheasants and game, which become a part of our food chain. There are dogs with jobs ranging across all kinds of areas; gundogs; agility dogs; herding dogs. They assist man in so many ways and are highly trained and enjoy their work beside their masters so much.

Dogs of the Working Group were originally bred to perform such jobs as guarding property, pulling sleds, and performing water rescues. They have been invaluable assets to man throughout the ages. The Doberman Pinscher, Siberian Husky, and Great Dane are included in this Group, to name just a few.

WORKING GUNDOGS

Dogs accompany the guns on a day's shoot and usually work with all manner of game, from rabbits and hares, to partridges, pigeons, ducks and pheasants. Many of our best loved-breeds were traditionally developed to help man in hunting. Labrador Retrievers gathered game in the field; Cocker Spaniels flushed and retrieved game; Pointers and Setters ranged over the fields helping us seek out birds and rabbits for the table. A great many still assist us in shooting and hunting today and are still very much part of our countryside sports.

11 http://www.bodyandmind.co.za/animalcentre/The_Purrfect_Crime_Fighter.html

HERDING

Along with hunting, herding is probably one of the oldest professions for dogs. There are as many dogs bred specifically for herding as there are forms of herding itself. Some breeds use what is called 'eye' – the tendency to stare down sheep. Dogs may be strong-eyed, medium-eyed, or loose-eyed. Border Collies are an example of a strong-eyed breed. An Old English Sheepdog, in contrast, does not have much eye. Dogs may use nipping or barking to move the sheep – Corgis are well known for their ability to dart in and nip the heels of cattle, for example. Other dogs were drovers, that is, they physically butt up against the stock to move them. Rottweilers and Bouviers are both used for this type of work.

Dogs have a fabulous ability to control the movement of other animals. A remarkable example is the low-set Corgi, perhaps one foot tall at the shoulders, which can drive a herd of cows many times its size to pasture by leaping and nipping at their heels. The vast majority of Herding dogs, as household pets, never cross paths with a farm animal. Nevertheless, pure instinct prompts many of these dogs to gently herd their owners, especially the children of the family!

LEOPARD TRACKING

When Claudia Schoene joined the Zoological Society of London as the project manager for their Amur Leopard Project, based in the Russian Far East, her Labrador dog, Tim, didn't realise that he was in for a career change, too. Tim, who had been with Claudia for nine years in Africa, had to adapt to the chilly climes of Vladivostok and be trained to find wild leopard scats for disease and DNA analysis.

In the Russian Far East, dogs have been used before to find poachers and tiger faeces. Tim had training sessions with dog trainer Linda Kerely near to the Lasovsky reserve in the south east of the Russian Far East. 'Tim has learnt to retrieve a perforated plastic bottle containing leopard scats, even when it is concealed under an upturned bucket,' said Claudia. 'I will keep training him now at home, returning for a further session in July. In August, we will go out into the forest and put Tim's training into practice.'

Despite the radical climate change, Tim seemed to have responded well to his training and he even had a regulation dog coat and matching booties to cope with the deep snow!

DOGS IN SPACE

Man's constant quest for explanations about, and subsequent exploration of space is well-documented. What should never be forgotten is the role held by dogs in the early days of space exploration. Their sacrifice paved the way for the beginning of the necessary understanding that has, in our time, led to comparatively safe space travel for an élite few.

Laika (which means 'barker' in Russian) was one such dog. She was a stray, thought to be a cross-bred, but mainly Siberian, husky and she was discovered on the streets of Moscow. Laika found herself at the Moscow Research Centre, where she was thought to be suitable for canine astronaut training. Russia, at that time was a main contender in the 'space race'. The use of dogs in space was seen as an opportunity to gain further knowledge about what would be needed to enable a human being to be fired into the unknown and survive.

Laika went through all the training required of her. She got used to being immobilised in the capsule of what would be Sputnik 2, while relying on battery-powered, life support systems that would not only feed her but also be essential for her oxygen and safety.

Sputnik 2 blasted off from the Soviet Union's Baikonur Cosmodome on 3 November 1957. Laika was the first animal to go into orbit. However, Sputnik 2 was not made for recovery: as the batteries of her life support ran down, so brave little Laika died. The capsule later fell into the atmosphere and burnt up on 14 April 1958.

Laika became world-famous and captured the imagination of nations. America called her little 'Muttnik' and the press told her story while questioning the morality of using dogs for such experiments. Forty years after her journey into space, the Moscow Research Centre where she was trained remembered her by unveiling a plaque in her honour.

In all, Russia launched thirteen other dogs into space to further their knowledge. They too should not be forgotten and deserve a mention here as brave little souls like Laika. Sadly, five of these dogs died in flight or at launch. When we next look up at the stars and wonder, we should also remember the dogs who helped mankind seek out new horizons and ultimately assisted in making space travel possible.

Dogs are dispatched into perilous and often unknown situations – think of the black-and-white pictures of dogs being rocketed to the moon – from there to war zones to safety checks – their lives are seen as more expendable than those of humans.

CHAPTER 5

Assistance Dogs –
Guide Dogs for the Blind,
Hearing Dogs for Deaf People,
Dogs for the Disabled,
Seizure Alert Dogs

'Until he extends the circle of his compassion to all living things, man will not himself find peace.'

DR ALBERT SCHWEITZER

Assistance dogs are specially trained to provide people who have physical, mental and hidden disabilities with the profound gift of improved access, mobility, independence and quality of life. Under the law they are not classified as pets and they are allowed in public places where normal pets are prohibited, such as shops, schools, restaurants, cinemas and tourist attractions. These dogs serve as the hands, ears, or eyes of their human partners and assist them by performing everyday tasks that would otherwise be difficult or impossible, as well as leading them away from danger. Think of the courage of the registered assistance dogs, such as Roselle, a Labrador, who led her blind owner to safety from the seventy-eighth floor of the World Trade Center before it collapsed on September 11 2001, or those who brought people out of the London Underground during the attacks of 7 July 2005. Other specially trained dogs are able to warn people with epilepsy of an oncoming attack minutes – sometimes hours – before it occurs. This allows the person time to take seizure blocking medication, to get to a safe place, or to call for assistance.

Assistance Dogs (UK) is an umbrella organisation for Canine Partners, Dogs for the Disabled, Hearing Dogs for Deaf People, Support Dogs and the Guide Dogs for the Blind Association. It is easy to distinguish between an assistance dog and a pet: an assistance dog is easily recognisable by the harness it wears and the special jacket with the Assistance Dogs UK logo.

GUIDE DOGS FOR THE BLIND

'A Guide Dog is almost equal in many ways to giving a blind man sight itself.'

MUSGRAVE FRANKLAND, ONE OF THE FIRST FOUR
BRITISH PEOPLE TO TRAIN WITH A GUIDE DOG

Whatever one's age, whatever the condition, sight loss causes a *huge* adjustment to everyday routines and activities. Above all, it can mean a severe loss of mobility. The Guide Dogs for the Blind Association helps, with the extraordinary partnership between guide dog and visually impaired owner at the core.

2006 saw the Association celebrate seventy-five years since the first working Guide Dog partnerships appeared on the streets of the UK. Three-quarters of a century later, the charity's dedicated team of staff, volunteers and supporters continue to provide freedom, mobility and independence for blind and partially sighted people. Every year, around 1,200 would-be Guide Dogs are born at home to the charity's brood bitches, specially chosen for their intelligence and temperament.

Volunteer puppy walkers introduce the young pups to the sights, sounds and smells of a world in which they will play such an important part. After just over a year the young dogs start their formal training, where they learn the skills needed to guide a blind or partially-sighted person. Training is rigorous – it has to be – and not all the young dogs make the grade. For the majority who do, the introduction to their new owner marks the start of a partnership that will last around six years.

The couple spend three weeks of intensive training with Guide Dogs' specialist staff before they are ready to face new, everyday challenges – the bond between Guide Dog and visually impaired owner has begun.[1]

There are currently around 4,700 guide dog partnerships in the UK. The reasonably short working life of a Guide Dog means a Guide Dog owner could have six or seven dogs during their lifetime. Today, the Guide Dogs for the Blind Association is the world's largest breeder and trainer of working dogs. Thanks to the work of dedicated staff and volunteers, some 21,000 blind and partially-sighted people have experienced the independence that a Guide Dog can bring. Retired dogs are offered to the homes that trained them as puppies, or given to homes best suited to well-behaved older dogs. Sooner or later, most Guide Dog users must face the possibility of retiring their dogs. Retirement can be difficult, whether someone has

1 Guide Dogs for the Blind's Embargo newsletter, 8 September 2005

worked a dog for a long time or has had it for only a few months. Naturally, it's hard to say goodbye to a longstanding partner and a friend you have come to rely on, day to day. Once retired, their visually impaired owner is given first option to keep the dog as a pet, or to place it among friends or family. If they are unable to do so, the option to place or keep the dog is then given to the dog's puppy raiser or to another suitably loving home.

Phyllis, a Guide Dog user, wrote,

> 'I have had three Guide Dogs, and they have all been attuned to my moods. If I am depressed, they seem to be; and if I am happy, they will reflect that, too. My first Guide Dog moved with me to Memphis, Tennessee. We didn't get back home to Nashville very often. Once, I remember, it was three years since we had been there. Yet every time we travelled back to Memphis, my dog would sleep until we were almost there. Then she'd wake up when we got near home! Also, she remembered that we used to live in Nashville, and when we'd go downtown, she'd always still stop at some of the places we used to go when we lived there! I found lots of old friends that way. This never ceased to amaze me how she could do that!' (2)

Robin Evans wrote about a time when he was crossing the road:

> 'My wife Wendy was with me so I relied on her to tell me that the road was clear and safe to cross.

2 Phyllis S. from http://paranormal.about.com/library/weekly/aa021201b.htm

'When she said, "OK," I gave Rascal the command to cross the road and he refused to move. Just then, out of the blue a car came roaring round the corner. Wendy had not seen it obviously and I didn't hear it as at the time it was too far away. But something had told Rascal that it was not safe and he just sat there ignoring my egging him on to move!

'Another time we were walking along a footpath when I wanted Rascal to take me to the kerb on the left. He refused and just stopped. I told him off as I thought he was being disobedient. The next second a bicycle came haring round the corner and obviously would have run Rascal and me down if he had not stopped.'

Finally, there was another occasion on which Rascal showed a profound intelligence. As Robin writes:

'We were at our local shops one day and rain was threatening, and I didn't know if we were going to make it home before it started. Well, we were about 150–200 yards from home and the skies opened. It was a terrible deluge. The rain was coming down with great force and at such an angle that it drove right underneath my shades, which I wear to protect my eyes and which also have side flaps to stop the wind, etc from getting into my eyes, which are extremely sensitive.

'It was coming down with such force that it not only knocked out the small amount of remaining sight I have in my right eye, it also affected my hearing, such was the torrential downpour. A couple of hundred yards doesn't seem much, but when you take our situation into *consideration, it is a very long way and I just didn't know if we were going to make it home safely. We had one road to cross, which is busy at times. There was no way I could hear the traffic coming and I definitely had no vision with which to help us by. So, I put all my trust in Rascal. He took me to the kerb and sat without my command to do so. I felt his head turning left and right on the harness as he was looking up and down the road.*

'Suddenly he was up and we were crossing the road and indeed at that time it was clear with no traffic coming. Rascal had waited until it was safe and took it upon himself to get us both home safely.

'There are no words to describe how I felt that day.'

GUIDE DOGS OF THE YEAR

Guide Dog Vaughn was named Guide Dog of the Year 2005 after transforming the life of his owner Susan Jones with his exceptional work. Susan described him as 'my hero'. The amazing Labrador-Retriever Cross was chosen to win the award after demonstrating his outstanding loyalty, devotion and work in guiding visually impaired Susan around Warrington, in Cheshire.

Susan, who is forty-four, also suffers from an occasional loss of hearing, which can strike without warning, often leaving her disorientated. On one occasion, Susan and Vaughn were walking through a shopping centre when she suddenly lost her hearing. Despite Susan feeling disorientated, Vaughn stopped and nuzzled her hand as if to reassure her. He then pushed Susan's hand with his nose to turn her back in the right direction, before continuing to guide her.

Susan said, 'Without Vaughn being by my side, I would have been stranded, unable to hear or see what was going on around me. I rely on my hearing to orientate myself and to lose it suddenly can be very frightening, but I know that Vaughn is here to help and guide me in the right direction. It is wonderful to have such a trusting working relationship with Vaughn and he is my hero!'

Guide dog Eamon was named as Life-Changing Guide Dog of the Year after making a huge difference to his owner, nineteen-year-old Stuart Beveridge. Stuart, from Lochgelly, in Fife, grew up only being able to see light and dark, and did not leave his house without his mother or father at his side. However, he now has the confidence to lead the normal teenage life that he's always wanted – all down to him being partnered with his first Guide Dog, Labrador-Retriever Cross Eamon.

He explained, 'Before Eamon came into my life, I didn't like going out on my own as I was scared that I'd get lost; now I know that I am not alone and there is someone looking out for me. Eamon and I are always going out to the shops, to meet my friends, or to the football with my dad.

'At school I always relied on my friends and teachers to take me everywhere but now Eamon can guide me – there's no excuse for being late!'

The extraordinary bond between Stuart and Eamon is easy to see, as Stuart is forever patting and talking to Eamon – 'He's like a best pal – my best friend,' says Stuart, 'he's so good natured and just brilliant!'

Guide Dog Vale was named Exceptional Work Guide Dog of the Year for helping her owner Nicola Cockburn to lead a more independent and varied life. Golden Retriever Vale has consistently worked beyond the call of duty as a devoted and willing companion to her owner. Nicola, who is twenty-seven and from Llandudno, Wales, began touring with a theatre company last year, primarily around Manchester and Glasgow, and for each town they visited, Vale had a new set of routes to learn. Despite there being only limited time to master the areas, Vale literally took it all in her stride and guided Nicola successfully from hotels to the theatres, local shops, bus stops and, most importantly, for Vale, to the park for a run.

'Vale is amazing, whenever we travel away from home she copes extremely well with any changes and is always willing to adapt to the new environment. Once we come home she remembers all of our old routes, including back to college when we haven't been for three months – she's amazing.'

Timber was named as Heroic Guide Dog of the Year after an act of bravery that saved his owner, Arthur Griffiths, from being seriously injured by a car that had gone out of control. Arthur and four-year-old Timber, from Crewe, in Cheshire, were waiting for Arthur's grandson to come out of Cub Scouts, when Timber began to pull Arthur away from where they were standing. Totally blind, Arthur did not realise what had happened when he suddenly heard a loud bang, until passers-by told him that Timber had just saved his life. What Arthur did not know was that two cars had crashed into each other, with one spinning off the road and landing near to where Arthur and Timber had been standing only seconds earlier.

Arthur commented: 'Timber is my hero and undoubtedly saved my life. If he had not moved us both further up the road, I dread to think what would have happened. Afterwards he just returned to normal and guided me home with my grandson – a true professional and my very special Guide Dog.'

HEARING DOGS FOR DEAF PEOPLE

Nearly nine million of the UK's population experience some degree of hearing loss, which equates to one person in every seven. Over 650,000 of these people are severely or profoundly deaf and could benefit from a Hearing Dog.

Like Guide Dogs for the Blind, Hearing Dogs also change lives by alerting their deaf owners to sounds that we take for granted, such as the doorbell, phones, smoke alarms, timers and so forth, providing greater independence, confidence and security. Most are selected from rescue centres or donated as unwanted pets.

Hearing Dogs for Deaf People was launched at Crufts Dog Show in 1982. Since then, they have continued to train dogs to alert deaf people to specific sounds, whether in the home, workplace or public buildings. To date, over 1,100 Hearing Dogs have been placed throughout England, Scotland, Wales, Northern Ireland and the Channel Islands.

Milly is eleven years old and has been with Glen Tallett, who is profoundly deaf, for over seven years. Glen and Milly have a very special relationship, which Glen explains in his own words:

'I am profoundly deaf, and because I have cerebral palsy, the combination with difficult facial and mouth muscles makes speech almost impossible. I am now thirty-eight years old. I spent most of my life in special schools and

later special units in college. My main ambition in adult life was to live independently.

'When I moved into my housing association bungalow near my parents, I knew that a Hearing Dog would be an important addition to my independence. When I first made my application for a Hearing Dog, my parents, as always, supported my decision, but Mum was very honest about not wanting the responsibility. I am a wheelchair user and I depend on my parents to assist me and to keep me in my own home. Also Mum didn't really like dogs.

'I met opposition everywhere. My relatives, friends and neighbours all said, "How will you exercise and look after a dog? You have enough problems looking after yourself." However, my GP, while concerned about the additional problems for my parents, was great in giving his support and the audiologist at the hospital also had confidence in my determination.

'Hearing Dogs for Deaf People took my application as a challenge to their expertise in training a dog to meet my special needs. With my difficult hand control, I had expected a small, short-haired, easy-to-handle Terrier. Instead, I met Milly, a medium size Springer Spaniel–Labrador crossbreed, already four years old.

'Milly's obvious desire to be needed and loved made her exceptionally sensitive and responsive to my needs and her intelligence was soon obvious when Jackie, her trainer, began training her to trot by my electric wheelchair without endangering herself or me. I now have an electric scooter; this would be too fast for Milly to run alongside me, so I bought one especially for its wide foot platform, which allows Milly to sit under my knees when taking her to the shops or the park.

'In addition to responding to the sound of my alarm clock, telephone, doorbell and smoke alarm, Milly learnt to pick up things that I might drop, to fetch things that I needed and alert people when I needed them.

'I also had a lot to learn, as I'd never had a dog before. At first, I worried – the same as I would have worried about a new baby – but my Hearing Dog trainers and placement officers were always there to answer my questions via the fax machine and Milly and I soon learned.

'At first, Milly wasn't keen on travelling by car – she quivered and whined. It took about six months for her to feel confident and secure about the car and now, just try keeping her away! The sound of Dad's car has new meaning for her, a family outing, or just shopping where she will get lots of attention and admiration. She has become quite a little celebrity locally, often seen travelling on the platform of my scooter and Hearing Dogs say that Milly has achieved a much higher level of understanding than anyone ever expected.

'Although my family and friends are very involved in our lives, Milly knows that she is my dog and that she works for me. Twice, we have been shopping in big stores when a fire alarm sounded and Milly immediately responds by telling me.

'Milly gives me confidence to live alone. She works for me and seldom, if ever, fails to alert me to everyday sounds. She collects mail and papers for me now without my asking her. I work at my computer desk and when she hears my printer working, she goes under my desk to the printer, takes out the paper in her mouth and either puts it on my lap or on my desk.

'Milly has changed my life and is a delight to everybody around her. People who were too embarrassed to talk to me before now always stop for Milly. Shopping takes hours because so many people want to stop and talk to Milly and they try to communicate with me. She is a wonderful example for Hearing Dogs.

'I could not be as independent or as confident without Milly; she accompanies me everywhere. In fact, if Milly could not go, then I would not go. With Milly I feel safe. I am not separated from the hearing world. I could write so much about the intelligent and sometimes funny things that she does. She is amazing. We are now two halves of one person. She is my ears.'

Regan has been a Hearing Dog for Elizabeth Hadden for just two years, but she has made an immense difference to her life and has almost certainly used her initiative and training to save her life. Elizabeth tells the story:

'To testify to her obedience and skill would be so easy – simply everyone who knows her marvels at her ability. She does everything that she was trained to do and I am privileged to have her as my companion.

'However, no amount of training can be congratulated for the natural instincts she possesses which, combined with this instruction, amounted to a near miracle which saved me from severe debility and possible tragedy. I will, *nevertheless, allow you to be the judge as I tell you this inspiring tale about my little friend.*

'During our daily walk through the local gardens, Regan suddenly jumped in front of me and lay down in the "danger position". At first, I thought she was playing with me and brought her back alongside me to continue our walk.

'Once again, she jumped up in front of me – as if to stop me walking – and lay down in the "danger position" again. Before I could react to her in my frustration at her nonsense, a large tree – uprooted by the fierce local winds during the previous day – crashed to the side of me across a bridge.

'The noise had alarmed her and she was protecting me. I was unable to take in all these events just at that moment. Eventually I realised that Regan's training coupled with her own inimitable canine resources, joined to avoid the situation that could have been tragic for me.

'I have had many dogs as family pets throughout my long life and appreciate that training can be useful in many situations. However, something extra special was involved here and that substance was used through my dog. I can do no greater thing, nor offer any greater praise to Regan, than to nominate her for Heroic Hearing Dog of the Year Award.'

Cavalier King Charles Spaniel Harry has been Pat Preston's Hearing Dog since July 1999, and in 2006, he won the prestigious Life-Changing Hearing Dog of the Year Award. This is Pat and Harry's story:

'Without doubt, Harry, my lovely Hearing Dog, has changed and enriched my life more than I can say. He has helped me so much, not only by working for me, but by enabling me to face the future with confidence about my deafness.

'Until my mid-forties I enjoyed perfect hearing, but after recovering from a virus, my family noticed that I was not responding to their conversation unless they were looking at me and that I was ignoring telephone calls and the doorbell. Plucking up my courage, I went to see a specialist, who confirmed that I had suffered severe hearing loss in both ears with a total loss of high sounds.

'Despite all the good advice from the Audiology Department, I found it almost impossible to tell people that I was now deaf, as I feared that I would be treated differently. I knew I could not bear it if people shouted at me or spoke in an exaggerated way and I was so reluctant to let go of my busy rewarding life as a fully hearing person.

'My husband often needed to travel abroad on business and as my children were grown up and had left home, I found myself becoming increasingly isolated. Sometimes, I would see a car drawing away from the house and realise that I had missed a friend's visit and on checking the answerphone would see that I had not heard several calls. I was worried that people would lose patience and give up calling.

'If I heard a strange noise in the house, my deafness meant that I could not tell where the sound was located, so I had to search each room, usually with an awful feeling of apprehension. Gradually, my house seemed to be the place where I was most stressed and anxious.

'Then Harry came into my life and I haven't looked back. Knowing that he will alert me to the doorbell, telephone and smoke alarm, and respond to any unusual noise has lifted all these worries away. I am so much more relaxed and able to enjoy my home again, feeling so much safer with him beside me.

'Harry loves working and it is wonderful to see him so happy when he alerts me. I can never feel miserable when he is around with his constantly wagging tail. The bond between us is so strong that he has alerted me to many extra things that he himself has noticed. When walking down a country lane, he alerted me to a car approaching behind us and he would not leave the kitchen when I left the tap dripping.

'I have to admit it was love at first sight when I was "introduced" to Harry. I just couldn't believe he was going to be mine. He is a very calm little dog, but can also be a bundle of fun. He is the most wonderful companion and thanks to him my confidence has grown enormously. Whenever we go out, he wears his burgundy coat and I am so proud of him that I no longer care that everyone will know that I am deaf. Accordingly, my life has become so much happier and easier.

'During our walks and shopping expeditions, I have noticed that people walking towards us see Harry and immediately start to smile. As we live in a town with tourists from the four corners of the earth, I have to say that the whole world seems to be a much brighter and

friendlier place. "Excuse me, but may I stroke your dog?"
is a question that I am asked often and I find myself
enjoying a chat with a complete stranger. Thanks to
Harry, I have met so many lovely people and experienced
nothing but kindness.

Pat's son originally contacted Hearing Dogs on her behalf
and every day she is grateful for that initial phone call which
heralded the start of her life with Harry. He is loved by
everyone and a relationship has been built with Pat's
husband – the entire family has benefited enormously
knowing that with Harry's help she can now cope so well in
her quiet world.

'It is hard to believe that almost seven years have passed
since Harry became my wonderful Hearing Dog. During
that time his work, help and loving companionship has
certainly been life-changing for me.

'Earlier this year, I had to attend a memorial service. I
knew there would be hundreds of people present, and as
this meant there would be a great shortage of space, I
reluctantly made the decision to leave Harry safely at
home. It was definitely the right decision for him but not
for me. How I missed his calm presence and support. I felt
so vulnerable, surrounded by people greeting each other,
wrapped around by noise but unable to hear a word,
hoping that no one would speak to me. Without Harry
beside me and without his coat explaining that I was now
deaf, I was completely lost and longed to return to the
safety of my home.

'This experience made me realise just how much I owe Harry. After my sudden hearing loss, feelings of panic and anxiety were a normal everyday way of life. Attending any function or going into a room full of people, even those I cared about most, was always a nightmare, something to dread and if possible avoid altogether. But now with Harry's support I feel so much more confident. People are always so pleased to see him, I walk into a room full of smiles and my fear disappears.

'Harry has a super-sense if I ever feel sad. He will sit beside me with his head on my knee or foot and it is such a comfort. He is my inspiration because he has one or two health problems himself, but he never lets it get him down. He's hungry for life and so full of fun.

'His work in the home has made all the difference to me. I have moved on from an isolated life to one in which each phone call is answered and visitors are once again welcomed when they call to see me. Loneliness has changed to busy days, friendship and new interests. With him beside me, I want to try new situations, so life is exciting again.

'One of the worse aspects of becoming deaf was knowing that my family were so worried about me and the thought of being a nuisance to everyone through mishearing. But having Harry has given me an independence which I thought was lost forever, and has taken that pressure away from them. Thanks to my lovely dog I have learnt to laugh at my mistakes. It is embarrassing but not the end of the world.

'Becoming a speaker for Hearing Dogs was a huge step

for me and something that would have been beyond my wildest dreams before Harry and I began our partnership. It gives me such pleasure to share my experiences of life with him. The groups we talk to all fall in love with him and I have met so many lovely people and benefited from so much kindness and interest. As an ex-teacher going into schools to visit a class or take an assembly is an absolute joy. My deafness ended my career so it is wonderful to have an opportunity to return to my world and to be surrounded by a sea of small faces loving every minute of Harry's company.

'I know I am the luckiest person in the world to have him. Harry has not only given me back my life, but created a wonderful new one for me. He makes me feel safe and so much more confident, and has brought me nothing but happiness. I am so proud of him and bless the day he was given to me.'

Profoundly deaf Sheila Walker has had her Hearing Dog Tess since April 2003, and she talks about how much impact Tess has had on her life.

'This is my narrative on how Tess has, and continues to change my life for the better. I dedicate this story to you, Tess. It is because of you I have a story to tell. My story begins in May 1999, a day etched on my mind never to be forgotten. I was at a school fête helping my partner Tony. It was a lovely summer's day, and never in my wildest dreams could I ever have imagined how my life was about to change. Suddenly, and without any warning

this happy carefree moment ended when I realised I couldn't hear. I had perfect hearing when I woke up and was deaf by 4pm. It's almost impossible to describe that moment. I felt I had fallen into deep water without knowing if I would resurface. I am aware life can deal some pretty bad cards – bereavement, divorce, crime and from one that knows I have climbed some tough mountains – but there is support and understanding from those that care.

'Deafness cannot be understood. It has an enormous social and emotional impact, like a pebble in a pond that makes lots of ripples. It affects family and friends – and life itself. Truly devastating for all concerned. The silent killer – deafness. I felt deeply depressed that this had happened to me. Completely and utterly shocked, my mind was full of dark negative thoughts, one of those "stop the world I want to get off" moments, only ten times worse. My deaf journey had begun. I was at rock bottom and felt like life had ended.

'It was all the little sounds that I missed: the indicator in the car, the cat flap, the sound of the bath running. I hated losing the independence of getting myself up in the morning. I found I couldn't relax because I knew I needed to wake up and might not hear the alarm clock.

'The care and support from my local hospital has been of the highest standard and it was through them that the suggestion of having a hearing dog was made to me. My first response was "What can a dog do?" and besides, I thought a dog would need walking, and walking would mean meeting people and that would require talking and I

81

*was deaf, so forget it – no dog! I've never been more
pleased to say how wrong I was.*

*'Tess came into my life at Easter 2003: a truly
beautiful, adorable, lovable little dog. Tess for me means
life after deafness. There is nothing I can't do with Tess by
my side. I have returned to work again, we go shopping
together; I am learning British Sign Language at college in
the evening. We take part in raising awareness of deaf
issues and are first in the queue to do a talk about the
wonderful bond we both share together. We have been stars
on our local radio station and have fought with
discrimination at being allowed to be together in a
courtroom. Together we can achieve anything. Through
Tess I have discovered my strengths and weaknesses, and
that anything is possible with her by my side.*

*'Tess has given me back independence, security and a
confidence I never had before. She is a part of me, and
taking her wherever I go is as automatic as picking up a
bag when I leave the house. As well as my hearing loss, I
suffer from vertigo. Tess senses an attack even before I do
and pesters me until she achieves her aim of getting me to
sit down safely.*

*'Tess is more than just my ears on legs and my
protector; Tess is always there for me and is everything
that is missing in terms of support and patience. Some
people give up trying to make themselves understood or tire
of listening – but Tess is always there, like a best mate.*

*'When the idea of a Hearing Dog was first suggested to
me, I thought it was a joke. Getting a dog was the last
thing on my mind. I wanted cochlear implants, the best*

surgeons money could buy. Now I wish I'd applied for a dog sooner, as I spent more than three hard years with my deafness before Tess came on the scene. I'm not running away any more. It's not my strength but Tess's. I thought my life was over when I lost my hearing, but I wouldn't have met Tess if it hadn't happened, and now I know which I'd rather have. I couldn't manage without her. I'd been through so many highs and lows in the last few years, but they're all highs now.

'She is just one remarkable, unique, life-changing, Hearing Dog. She has without a shadow of doubt changed mine. Tess, from the bottom of my heart, I thank you. If a genie was to appear now with a lamp and ask me, "Hearing Dog or hearing?" – no choice … come on, Tess – WALKIES!'

Golden retriever Luke has been Lynne Swarbrick's Hearing Dog since December 2004 and she spoke frankly about how much her life has changed since he has been there.

'I know in my heart how much Luke means to me and how he has totally changed my life for the better. He has brought so much happiness and love into my life. My name is Lynne. I'm forty-seven and since the age of twenty-six I have been slowly going deaf due to an illness called neurofibromatosis. The condition has caused tumours to grow on my hearing nerves. Five years ago, I had an operation to remove a tumour and this left me profoundly deaf, in a silent world, and as this happened, for the first time in my life, I found myself living alone. It

was a tremendous shock. I had lived most of my life hearing and around hearing people, and suddenly I was alone within my silent bubble. I felt like giving up, life was not worth living. I tried to fight it, but it felt like there was a black cloud hanging over me. I thought long and hard about the options and in the end decided to apply for a Hearing Dog.

'The two-year wait was very hard and scary, especially at night. I couldn't hear a thing but could feel vibrations and this made me very jumpy when it happened. I couldn't sleep. I was continually going to the top of the stairs sniffing, to make sure the house wasn't on fire. I also experience tinnitus quite badly, and would feel the vibrations of the noises in my head and think someone was trying to break into the house.

'Finally, I went to the training centre to meet Luke. I remember it as though it were yesterday. He was so beautiful: he was gentle and had the biggest, softest eyes I have ever seen. I am unsteady on my feet but with Luke by my side I felt much steadier. Well, that was it: I was in love. At the end of his training, I took him home with me. I felt so relaxed to have him with me. I took him out for his first walk and really enjoyed it. Luke is such a therapeutic dog. I worked with him and he just got better and better. I am so proud of him; even now as I am writing this, I am filled with so much emotion I could cry.

'Before I had Luke I was often thought to be ignorant because people didn't know I was deaf. Deafness is a silent disability. Now, however, when I am out, people know that I am deaf – Luke's coat tells them – and everyone is so friendly now. Luke loves everyone and is so gentle with older people and children, it's as though he knows when people have special needs. Everywhere we go, he spreads sunshine into everybody's life, and I feel blessed to have the joy of Luke in my life. He is my hero and has changed my life beyond my wildest dreams. I am so happy and content, I feel safe now that he is by my side always and he never leaves me.

'I love him more and more, and with every passing day the bond between us gets stronger. The day that Luke came into my life, the black cloud that surrounded me changed into beautiful golden light. He's opened up my silent world and given me the strength to carry on. He is my best friend, my ears, my guide at night; he is my world.'

Ian Joyce has had Hearing Dog Hettie since June 2005 and the impact she has had on his life in that short time is quite extraordinary. He takes up the story:

I have been deaf since birth but during my adult life have worn two hearing aids. However, from 1998 onwards, I started to have major problems with my ears which, despite having operations, resulted – in 2002 – in my not being able to wear my hearing aids again.

'This was a huge shock and one which I wasn't able to cope with: the resulting depression led to me leaving secure employment due to my mental state. It would be no exaggeration to say that I no longer cared about life as I didn't think I was able to take a part in the hearing or deaf *world. The large number of lacerations on my arms, as well as suffering from malnutrition, bore testimony to this and resulted in my being placed under the care of the local area Mental Health Team. Life was basically pills and weekly and monthly visits to various healthcare professionals. The only communication I had with the outside world was with these people; I never left the house for social purposes, as I was scared of communicating, so scared that I would become too anxious at the thought. Indeed, it was only through Social Services volunteers that I could get out to my appointments.*

'One morning, while waiting for my social worker, I noticed a leaflet for Hearing Dogs for Deaf People. I asked about this, as I loved animals. It was decided that it was a good idea and I submitted an application. There followed a home visit by Hearing Dogs to discuss my application and I was accepted but was told of the waiting time to receive a dog. Life followed the same routines, although I did feel nervous at the thought, I felt more positive as life seemed to have a goal.

'In April 2005, I received a letter asking me to visit the northern training centre to meet Hettie – a Norwegian Buhund. "A what?" I thought, so I looked it up on the Internet and remember running round the room screaming "yes!" as the dog I would always want is a Husky and Buhunds looked very similar. I visited Hettie and fell in love. She was so pretty, so different, but like me had some confidence issues so I thought, what a great team, that we could complement each other and develop our confidence together.

'Hettie came to live with me on 25 June 2005, and I wouldn't be honest if I said that the eight months since she has been here have been easy. Indeed, it has been one of the most intense periods I have known. There has been much laughter where there was previously none and some tears of frustration.

'However, such things as Hettie chewing the remote control pale into insignificance compared to the rewards she has brought. Yes, she has enabled me to be aware of sounds that I no longer hear, such as the doorbell, alarm clock and so on, but the relationship is much deeper than that. She has given me companionship, independence, peace of mind; but in my view the greatest things she has given me are trust and the removal of fear.

'Before I no longer trusted people. I couldn't go out as I was fearful of people talking to me, fearful of not being understood or being misunderstood. I would walk with my head down, not wanting to make contact with people. Also, my mannerisms were of hostility as I was also angry at the world. Now I feel ten feet tall. In the last eight months I have never talked to so many people – whether walking Hettie in the parks, nature reserve, shopping in the supermarket, walking in the city centre. The things I couldn't do before, like go for a cup of coffee and feel relaxed, I now look forward to. I have made some new friends and found some new interests. I feel people welcome us now, where before I thought they would turn me away. When she wakes me up in the morning I see the love in her eyes and her tail wags; it fills me with joy and thoughts of how lucky I am. I feel like a part of the human *race instead of being estranged from it. I no longer hate my world or my life. All of this is due to Hettie and Hearing Dogs for Deaf People.*

'Hettie is truly a life-changing dog as she has given me back the most precious thing we have, which is life. Whether Hettie succeeds or not in this nomination, no one can take that away from us.'

Hearing Dog Garry was Brian Wallis's own pet dog when he decided he needed the help of a Hearing Dog. Garry was subsequently trained to alert Brian to sounds and here he tells in his own words what a difference Garry has made since he has become a Hearing Dog.

'I found life very frustrating and felt like I was in a black hole where I was getting deeper and deeper into the dark. I was all on my own. I stopped going out and lost contact with a lot of people. Due to this, among other things I became very depressed and was prescribed medication. I had lost my confidence and started to find it increasingly hard to communicate with people and so started to shut them out. When friends and family came, I would close my eyes and pretend to be asleep, the thought of trying to talk to people was unbearable and with everyone trying to talk to me at once, well, I just couldn't do it. The simplest things became a task, like going to the doctors or the hospital. I couldn't hear when I was being called and so would miss my turn. You wouldn't believe even crossing the road: one minute there would be no cars and so I would start to cross, then from nowhere out would pop a

motorbike. It just felt like I went from being somebody to nobody: because I couldn't hear people, they just started to ignore me and so I guess I began to do the same. There is no greater pain than being in a room full of people but being alone. It was like living in a box.

'I have had some serious health problems over the last few years which have left me with depression and am now disabled. To get around, I have to use crutches or a wheelchair. I wasn't looking to have a dog but Garry arrived because someone my son knew was going to take him to a rescue centre as they couldn't cope with him any more.

'We were together twenty-four hours a day and our bond was beginning to grow. This has made me go out and buy an electric scooter so I could take him for his walks. He would want to help me whatever I was doing in the house or garden, and he showed me he had more to offer, which is when Hearing Dogs came in.

'While I waited to see if they would train Garry, he was doing everything that was asked of him and more. Anything I dropped, he would pick up. He was always looking for something to do all the time. Then the news came that I had been waiting for: he had been accepted for training. Being without Garry for four and a half months was hard for me because we had got so close. I went back to not going out [or] only to the doctors or hospital. Eventually, I got the news that Garry had passed and would be coming home.

'When he arrived home, we started to work together. When he had his burgundy coat on, people who we did not know started to stop us. Some people said they did not know I was deaf. We started going out a little further and soon I noticed the change in people with Garry in his burgundy coat. At the hospital, I would no longer miss my turn, again Garry in his coat seemed to remind them. In the shops, people were giving me more time and space. Because he is there, people seem to talk to me directly. This may seem a small thing, but to me it's great. Sometimes, I am sure people thought I was being rude but I could not hear them. In the house, I no longer have to sit looking out the window waiting for the ambulance to pick me up. I can be doing other things. I can always rely on Garry to tell me because he is trained to do many things. He lets me know if someone is calling me, or the phone or doorbell is ringing. Again, small everyday things but for me it brings me more out of the box and into the real world.

'Garry does so many things for me as well as his soundwork. He puts washing in the machine, rubbish in the bin, picks up things, helps me to get out of bed. He gets my shoes and clothes, and he has now started to bring my wheelchair to me. He will open and close the fridge door.

'Garry is bright and cheerful. Working or not, inside or out, he always wants to please. I never go out without Garry. He is my ears and sometimes my eyes. He is my best friend and I couldn't see myself without him. Sometimes, I look back and wonder how I coped. I think that's how I became depressed as I was scared to do most day-to-day things, but now with Garry I can do almost anything.

'I have only had Garry as a Hearing Dog for a short time, but so many things have changed because of it. I am *beginning to get my confidence and independence back, bit by bit. Life is on the up. My box is getting smaller as more doors open.'*

DOGS FOR THE DISABLED

Shop assistants in Inverness are used to a small black-and-white Collie Cross with spotty paws running up for help to lift heavy goods off the shelves and into her mistress's shopping trolley. Gypsy is the second carer dog to look after Judy Westwater, who has severe fibromyalgia – a chronic condition that causes pain and soreness in muscles, tendons and ligaments plus profound exhaustion.

Gypsy is at Judy's side twenty-four hours a day, seven days a week: 'She answers the phone, loads and unloads the washing machine, stands by the shower in case I need help and takes my socks off for me.' During the night, Gypsy helps Judy turn over and in the mornings, she helps her out of bed.

Judy trained Gypsy herself and was then assessed by Support Dogs to make sure she could do everything Judy needed (Support Dogs also train disability dogs and seizure alert dogs). Social Services had offered Judy a human carer, but she refused – 'I always had more in common with animals than people' – which is not surprising as she relates in her book *Street Kid* (Harper Element, London, 2006) that she was abused by her spiritualist-preacher father. Starved and tortured, she became a feral child, roaming the streets of Manchester and later Johannesburg, after her father abducted her and took her to South Africa. In her teens her life turned around when she found a home with Wilkie's Circus, tending the animals and later working as a trapeze artist.

Her fibromyalgia was diagnosed in 1991: 'I'd always had aches and pains but they became much worse when my husband died. The doctors said it is often linked to a traumatic childhood and stress. I couldn't function as well as I do without Gypsy. She gives light to my life.'[3]

Chocolate Labrador Yogi, the 'guardian angel' of Daniel George of Hebburn, in Tyne and Wear, was nominated by Dogs for the Disabled for the Friends For Life parade at Crufts 2006. Twelve-year-old Daniel suffers from a severe condition called Duchenne Muscular Dystrophy, which affects and limits every aspect of his life. As a result, he is one of only three children in the UK to have an Assistance Dog trained especially for him as part of the Dogs for the Disabled children's project. Three-year-old Yogi has improved Daniel's confidence and independence so much that he no longer has to rely on other people to help him with everyday tasks, such as getting undressed or turning off his bedroom light.

'I feel like I'm trapped in a box and I can't get out,' said Daniel, but in the six months he and Yogi have been together, he has found a best friend: 'I just love him. He puts his face up to mine, and he wags his tail and makes me feel happy. He's so clever in the things that he does. Now I feel like I've always got a friend. I'm unsteady on my feet and I can easily fall. Yogi's been specially trained to bark so that Mum will hear and come to help me at any time of the day or night. That makes me feel safe and, for the first time in ages, I can do things by myself.'

When he was born, Daniel appeared to be completely

3 Health Notes: A Woman's Best Friend, *The Mail on Sunday*, *You* Magazine, p. 70, June 2006

healthy, but even at an early age his mother, Mary, suspected something was wrong. She explains: 'Daniel wasn't like his elder brother and parts of his development didn't seem right. He would sleep all the time and wouldn't sit up like a normal baby. As he grew older he did learn to walk but just couldn't manage stairs or push himself up from a sitting position.' Despite tests showing nothing, Mary eventually found a child orthopaedic specialist willing to listen and he helped to get Daniel diagnosed. She continues:

'When we were told Daniel had Duchennes I was left feeling absolutely crushed. For two weeks I went around in a daze; it's just too horrible to think that your son is going to be disabled and his life is going to be so limited. Worse still, that you can't protect him from what he's going to go through.

'Inside I was raging, I couldn't help thinking "Why us?" But you have to tell yourself: "I am going to do everything in my power to make sure that my son has what he needs to make his life as good as it can be." Having a child with a disability has an affect on the whole family. Sometimes, I need to do more for him than for his brother and sister, and that can be extremely hard for them to understand. Your emotions vary so much – you have good days when you cope really well and then the bad days when you just get so low and feel that the world is against you.'

For Daniel, life has become increasingly difficult. When he was ten, he hardly needed his wheelchair but now, two years later, his disability affects him more each day. He can't get himself undressed without assistance, and is unable to get out of a chair without someone helping him. Last year was probably the hardest year yet as it became clear that he would have to move to a new bedroom downstairs. He continues his story: 'I was really depressed when I had to move downstairs. It made me realise I was disabled and that life is going to be very different from my brother's and sister's life.'

Mary is still as determined as she was the day she found out about Daniel's condition. 'Even when Daniel's in bed, you don't stop thinking about ways to help him. I'll spend hours on the Internet looking at services available to him. That's how I found out about Dogs for the Disabled.' Through a US organisation, Mary saw that Dogs for the Disabled were looking to start a new UK project to help disabled children.

'My heart leapt when I heard. I knew there were projects helping disabled adults in the UK, but I thought that there was nothing for children. Our pet cat had recently died, and he had been such a friend to Daniel. He used to sit on his bed or curl up on his lap, and Daniel really missed the company.'

Soon after Mary's enquiry, the family found themselves taking part in an information day at Dogs for the Disabled, and it was there that Daniel met his new best friend. He explains: 'I remember when they brought Yogi in. This handsome dog just came up to me and wagged his tail and snuffled his nose into my hands. He was just brilliant. I hoped that I'd get a dog just like Yogi.'

Mary continues: 'I couldn't believe it when we got the call to say we'd been accepted onto the pilot project! Even more so when they told me that they thought Yogi would be the right dog. It was as if it was all meant to be.'

Soon afterwards Daniel and Yogi started their training and Mary believes that it was a real turning point for the whole family. Over the next few weeks, and with the help of a Dogs for the Disabled instructor, Daniel, Mary and Yogi began to form a team. 'Daniel loved Yogi, but emotionally he was still very unsteady and I just prayed it was all going to work. Day by day, Yogi started to work his special magic.'

'Yogi sleeps in Daniel's room so he is the first thing Daniel sees in the morning, and he is there in the night if Daniel should wake up. That wagging tail brightens everyone's mood.' So now, when Daniel goes to bed, so does his dog. Yogi can help him get ready for bed by opening the bathroom door, then helping him get undressed and even turning off the light switch once Daniel has got into bed. Even if Daniel's duvet should fall off in the middle of the night, Yogi makes sure that it's back over Daniel in a matter of seconds.

After six months, Daniel wouldn't be out without him: 'I feel like Yogi has helped me to be myself again. If I can get dressed and undressed with Yogi's help it means that I don't have to ask my mum for everything. I'm twelve years old and I don't want to have to rely on other people all the time, especially for simple things like getting up in the morning or fetching the TV remote. Yogi never says, "In a minute, Daniel," and never tuts or frowns.'

People react to Daniel in a different way, too. As Mary explains, this will help boost his confidence:

'When you're walking down a street with a child in a wheelchair, people don't know how to react. They look away or give you a sympathetic look – it feels horrible. I've

noticed a difference since Yogi's been coming everywhere with us. People smile and they want to talk and find out about this specially trained dog. They talk to Daniel, too, and that's making him feel more accepted. He volunteers to go out now rather than stay in the safety of his room. Having an Assistance Dog helps in so many different aspects of everyday life.

'Yogi is like a new member of the family, and we all love him. Disability affects every member of the family and it can leave you feeling sad and negative. Yogi hasn't cured that, but he has become a new and positive focus for the family. Daniel has a new friend and helper, his brother and sister have a rough-and-tumble playmate and I have someone that makes me smile.' [4]

At fourteen, Jamie was just like any other teenager, going to school and playing football with his mates. He was starting to enjoy some of the independence that goes with being a young adult – his local paper round meant that he even had his own pocket money and he dreamt of a career in the Army when he left school. But Jamie's life was to change forever when a car hit him as he cycled around his hometown in Devon. He sustained massive head injuries and spent the next year in hospital, rehabilitating. When he finally returned home, he was living a life from a wheelchair.

While he had looked forward to the day he could return home, Jamie found the reality was far more difficult than anyone could have prepared him for. Everything seemed so

4 'Yogi: Smarter than the average dog!', Newshound, reproduced by permission of Dogs for the Disabled

frustrating; he needed help with so much and it was difficult to do even the simplest things, such as getting dressed or manoeuvring around the house in his wheelchair. Worst of all, he had been away from school for such a long time that when he returned, he had to start back in a lower year. His friends had moved on and he could no longer join them on the school field for a game of football or at social gatherings after school. It made him feel even more isolated and alone.

His mother, Sharon, could only stand by and watch as her son became even more withdrawn.

> 'I used to say to him, "What can we do to help?" and always Jamie would tell me that he would like a dog, something that he could look after and call his own. I didn't know what to do, but the thought kept preying on my mind that a dog might just help.
>
> 'It was when Jamie was nearly seventeen that we heard about Dogs for the Disabled. Immediately we thought this had to be the answer. Jamie wrote to the charity explaining how he thought a dog could help him and shortly afterwards we received a visit from an instructor, who agreed that Jamie would be an ideal candidate.'

A few months later, Jamie received a call from his instructor saying that they thought they had a suitable dog. Kandy visited Jamie at his home to see how they took to one another and, in Jamie's words, 'it was love at first sight'. 'Kandy came straight up to me and put her front paws on the side of my wheelchair – I couldn't believe this beautiful dog was going to be mine.'

Kandy has now been part of Jamie's life for six years: 'From the moment we started training my life has changed. Looking back on the time before I had her, I know that really I had lost the will to live. Because of her, people no longer see my wheelchair, but they see her and they want to talk to me, and of course make a fuss of Kandy. I think Kandy has played a huge part in me accepting my situation.'

At home Kandy is able to do a huge amount to help Jamie. Not only does she open and close the doors around the house, she will also bring him the phone and will help unload the washing machine and get his things out of the tumble dryer. She has given him back a sense of independence and confidence that disappeared after the accident.

> 'One of my most nerve-racking moments was starting an HND in Business Management and Agriculture at college, and I'm not sure how I would have coped without Kandy. I didn't know anyone and it was my first time living away from home in the student halls. But as soon as we got there everyone wanted to meet Kandy and pretty soon we had friends all around campus. Without Kandy, I think I would have continued to feel different and isolated. The fact that she can help me with practical tasks as well as give me companionship is a key part of our relationship.'

Kandy goes everywhere with Jamie. At college, she would sit quietly at his feet during lectures, ready to pick up anything he dropped or help retrieve a book from the lower shelves in the library. With Kandy always on hand to help, Jamie was able to enjoy his independence just like the other students at college.

Jamie passed his HND last summer and since leaving he is

doing something that he really enjoys and is using the skills he gained in college. Working at the Barn Owl Trust (www.barnowltrust.org.uk) in Devon for three days a week, he is helping a team of specialists to find out more about this beautiful and rare species by registering the sightings of the birds in the area and examining their pellets to help understand more about their diets. Kandy lies faithfully at his feet while he works and has also become a valued member of the team. On the other days, Jamie helps out his mum at the local school, where she teaches children with special needs. As she says, 'Jamie and Kandy are a real asset in helping the children to learn. Jamie is able to help the children with their reading and maths. He's a very good listener and they really enjoy having him to help out.' She jokes that she always knows that the children are going to be better behaved when Jamie and Kandy are working. 'The children know that if they get all their work done, they can go and play with Kandy. Not surprisingly, they all work very hard to make sure they can give her a cuddle at the end of the lesson!'

It is perhaps Jamie's mum's words that best sum up the pair's relationship: 'Kandy has changed all our lives, but most of all Jamie's. First and foremost, she has given him a reason to live. I'd say she's saved his life.'[5]

SEIZURE ALERT AND SUPPORT DOGS

Tony has had epilepsy since 1989, having her first seizure when she was in hospital following a bad asthma attack, and having

5 *Newshound*, issue no. 3, 21 February 2003, reproduced by permission of Dogs for the Disabled

had around twelve seizures a week before she found out about Seizure Alert Dogs through the British Epilepsy Association.

In 1995 she was partnered with her first Seizure Alert Dog, Rupert, who gave her a reliable warning many minutes prior to an attack, reducing the danger of injury. Since being partnered with a Seizure Alert Dog, Tony's seizure frequency has reduced to around three a week, which she puts down to the confidence the dog has given her, putting her back in control.

Tony had been told that she and her husband would never be able to have children. However, in September 1999, she discovered that she was pregnant and Rupert's warning reduced the risk of injury to both Tony and the unborn baby. Tony had to stay in hospital for three weeks when Grace was born – naturally, Rupert stayed with her.

In October 2000, it was decided that after many years of working Rupert should retire. Tony was introduced to Caley, and both Tony and Caley took to each other. Although beginning work with a second dog was strange for Tony, while Caley was in the very early stages of Seizure Alert Training, Tony realised just how much she relied on Rupert's warning. Caley qualified as dog number 100 at the end of April 2001 and he, too, gives Tony a reliable alert before a seizure, allowing her to continue to look after Grace and attend all the usual places that a new mother would frequent. Caley accompanies Tony and Grace to the toddler groups and swimming pool, where he is accepted by everyone.

Rupert now lives close by with some friends of Tony's and is extremely happy in his retirement. To sum it up in Tony's own words: 'I used to have epilepsy with a little bit of life, now I have a life with a little bit of epilepsy.'

Interestingly, many epileptics can attest that their own family pet dogs are aware of an on-coming seizure. Julie Arrowsmith phoned into a BBC Radio Manchester programme on which I appeared while discussing this book, and said that her dog naturally and without any training acts really peculiarly, alerting her family to her being about to have a fit. It is this instinct in dogs that is harnessed and honed to produce specially trained Seizure Alert animals.

Support Dogs is dedicated to improving the quality of life for people with epilepsy and people with disabilities by training dogs to act as efficient and safe assistants. Support Dogs trains dogs to assist and support their disabled owners with their specific disability. Each dog is taught specific tasks for his owner's needs, enabling the disabled person to lead a fuller and more independent life. As a registered Assistance Dog, a Support Dog is able to accompany his owner at all times. Three types of Support Dog training are offered: Seizure Alert, Disability Assistance and Medical Assistance.

Seizure Alert Dogs are trained to detect the signs of an imminent seizure and to warn their owners, giving them enough time to get to a place of safety. The dogs can provide their owners with an accurate warning of between twenty and forty-five minutes. The type and length of warning each dog can give remains consistent so that the person knows exactly how long they have before the seizure happens.

The way in which the dogs warn their owner varies from one dog to another. Warning may be in the form of a bark or whine, or the dog may jump up or paw the owner. Dogs that are in seizure alert training must not have seen a seizure previously, so Support Dogs will not train the owner's pet dog. Instead, they are selected from rescue centres. Each dog is carefully chosen to ensure they are of the appropriate temperament and are 'people orientated'. They need to be confident and sociable, as well as able to undertake the work of a Support Dog.

Given the right temperament, most breeds can be trained. Support Dogs has identified traits in some dogs that make them more suitable for this type of work and these dogs are more responsive to seizure activity. Each dog is trained with its new owner so that they can learn to identify the owner's specific seizure activity. It is not clear how the dogs identify when a seizure is about to occur, but it is thought that they may pick up on unique signs of seizures – physiological or behavioural changes – that the people themselves and those around them are not aware of. These could include pupils dilating, or changes in facial expressions or colour.

At the end of 2001 Louise was partnered with Archie and it totally transformed her life. Louise has epilepsy that conventional drugs could not control, leaving her and her family living with the fear of an attack striking at any moment. Before being partnered with Archie, she was having around twenty seizures a day. Since their training was completed, she now has several seizure-free days in a row. Her epilepsy restricted all their lives and she was unable to carry out everyday tasks, such as making a cup of tea, or taking a bath without fear of injury.

Archie has transformed Louise's life by giving her a warning of ten minutes before a seizure. This warning means that she is able to live as full a life as possible. When she is out shopping,

Archie's warning allows her the time to find a medical room in a local shop so that her seizure can pass in safety and privacy.

Similarly, Gillian has had epilepsy for thirty-six years and the medical profession had been unsuccessful in finding a method of controlling her seizures. Nine years ago, she was told that she had another medical condition, which increased the frequency of the attacks.

'In 1996 I was living in South Africa when I heard about Seizure Alert Dogs. I knew I could only be assessed for the training programme if I lived in England. When my husband died, I returned to England to live and contacted Support Dogs Charity. After completing and returning the application form, assessments and medical reports, they told me that I might be a suitable candidate. Soon afterwards, Support Dogs telephoned to say that they had a small black dog named Harvey and would I be interested? I could hardly believe it!

'Harvey and I bonded straightaway – I knew we were meant for one another. He wasn't a fancy breed; in fact, he had been selected from a rescue centre. We underwent a total of six weeks intensive training and eight months later, Harvey qualified as a Seizure Alert Dog.

'Since then, having him as an "early warning system" has almost reduced my seizure frequency to nil except when my other medical condition flares up. Also, I have regained my self-confidence and live a much better quality of life. Harvey knows before I am going to have a seizure and he looks after me. My doctor is now reducing my medication because she believes Harvey is my remedy.

'Where I go, Harvey goes! I can't imagine what life would be like without him. He's my best friend and my life has taken on a new meaning with him by my side.'

OTHER ASSISTANCE DOGS

Support Dogs also train dogs to provide assistance to their owners in other ways. Medical assistance dogs are trained to meet the needs of people with medical conditions such as hypoglycaemia (diabetes), agoraphobia and Menière's disease. The dogs can help by bringing the person their medication, or by getting help, or pressing an alarm if the person becomes ill.

Disability Assistance Dogs are often the client's own pet dogs, who are trained to help their owner with everyday activities. From the beginning of the training, the dog and client work together to teach the dog tasks such as opening and closing doors, switching lights on and off, loading and unloading the washing machine, picking up, fetching and carrying objects. They can also be trained to help their owner to dress and they provide their owner with stability when walking.

DOGS AND DIABETES

Now and then, animal owners call the Diabetes UK Care line with stories of their pets (including a cockatoo!) warning them of their 'hypos'. Whenever there is more insulin in the body than is needed Hypos (Hypoglycaemia or low blood glucose) occur. It is usually uncomfortable rather than dangerous, but occasionally blood glucose goes so low that the brain runs out of fuel and ceases to work properly. Confusion, irritability, even unconsciousness, can result. A severe hypo leaves the person with diabetes unable to help him or herself and needing help from someone else – which is where Assistance Dogs have been trained and where other pets have stepped in.

The *British Medical Journal* (BMJ) even published an article along these lines in December 2000, with the snappy headline of 'Non-invasive detection of hypoglycaemia using a novel, fully biocompatible and patient friendly alarm system'. This alarm system consisted of dogs who seemed to warn their owners when their blood-glucose levels were falling low via various methods, including barking, door scrabbling and even preventing their owner from leaving the house until the hypo had been dealt with. One of the three dogs studied was a nine-year-old mongrel called Candy, who would run and hide whenever her owner was hypo – often before her owner was even aware of it – and would only re-emerge once she had eaten some carbohydrate.

Astonishingly, the research team found that of the dogs living with people with diabetes, over one third show various behavioural changes just before and when their owners are going hypo. The report in the *BMJ* also suggested that dogs could be affected by changes in smell – possibly due to sweating, a common symptom of hypos. Other hypo symptoms that may alert the dogs include muscle tremors and changes in behaviour – perhaps the owners do not respond to their four-legged-friends in their usual way. Because of this, some dogs are trained to identify hypo-warning symptoms in their owner. Support Dogs is a Sheffield-based charity that trains 'seizure alert' dogs for people with epilepsy.

'It's a lengthy process to teach dogs to detect the minute

physiological changes that occur in someone with epilepsy,' says head trainer, Rita Howson. 'Unfortunately, little research has been done into teaching dogs to detect hypos, but we are currently exploring extending our work to specifically train dogs for this. At present, though, while a pet may pick up on certain signs, there is no guarantee they will always respond to their owner's hypo, so people with diabetes shouldn't rely on their pets for this.'

However, just because a pet can't be a reliable hypo warning system, it doesn't mean they are unable to provide many other advantages for people with diabetes. 'It's a known fact that dogs are beneficial to cardiovascular health, which in turn is important to people with diabetes,' says Chris Laurence. 'And irrespective of who takes whom for a walk, physical activity helps to control your diabetes by reducing blood-glucose levels and helping you maintain a healthy weight.'

'Keeping any pet is generally calming,' he adds. 'Stroking it helps to reduce stress, which lowers blood pressure – again, important for people managing their diabetes.[6]

6 http://www.diabetes.org.uk/

CHAPTER 6

Animals and War

'Man has done a lot to make himself dangerous and animals get the worst of all of it. But then, man too is an animal.'

DON VAN VLIET

Until I saw the 2006–7 Animals' War exhibition at the Imperial War Museum (see http://www.iwm.org.uk), I never realised the extent to which animals have been (and still are) serving and dying alongside our armies during times of war: from glow worms that lit the soldiers' maps to carrier pigeons who saved many a boat in distress, to horses, donkeys, oxen, mules, camels and the present-day sniffer dogs and landmine-finding rats, their endearing personalities brought true affection and humour to the most desperate military situation.

In World War II, over 500,000 carrier pigeons were used by Britain's armed forces and secret service organisations, with about 20,000 of them killed in action. One of the bravest,

Mary of Exeter, survived a partly shot-off wing, a savage attack by a hawk and a neck wound so severe she had to wear a collar to support her head. Nevertheless, she completed five years of service for Britain, earning a People's Dispensary for Sick Animals (PDSA) Dickin medal – the Victoria Cross for animals[1]. Pigeons brought the first news of Wellington's victory at the Battle of Waterloo in 1815 and of the success of the D-Day landings in June 1944, while dogs have also been used for sending messages, as they can cover ground three times faster than a person on foot, as well as being able to see at night time and in inclement weather. Dogs have also been used to guard military personnel and property, locate injured soldiers, track down enemy insurgents and sniff out explosives. More recently rats and pigs have been trained to clear minefields and the dolphin's sensitive sonar exploited to identify mines in the Persian Gulf.

In her book, *The Children's War* (2005), Juliet Gardiner writes poignantly about the anguish members of the public faced when their horses were called up for World War I (the first part of the war relied on real horsepower before tanks were used) and recalls 'the sadness of one rough-looking man, whso came in with two cart horses and stayed half an hour patting them and giving them sugar'.

Of course, these owners had no idea of the atrocities to which they were committing their beloved animals – eight million horses were believed to have died in World War I. But most of them perished not from enemy fire but from cold, disease or starvation, so famished were they that they resorted

---

1 http://www.thisislocallondon.co.uk/display.var.852833.0.meet_jake_the_77_hero_dog.php

to chewing other horses' hairless or ate each other's rugs. Suffice to say, few returned home.[2]

It is estimated that a staggering 16 million animals served during World War I. By 1916 alone the warring nations had raised 103 cavalry divisions with over one million horses. Despite increasing mechanisation and advances in technology, animals have continued to play their part in the front line. Mules, elephants, camels, horses and other beasts have transported men and materiel in difficult terrain. By 1918, the British army was using over 800,000 horses, mules, camels, donkeys and oxen. Nearly 500,000 pack animals died in the War. Today the army has only one mule, Alfie, on its strength.[3]

Animal mascots were popular, too, and were used during the war, demonstrating bravery and loyalty, and earning the affections of their human counterparts. Dogs and horses were the most common mascots for regiments, but mascots ranged from hens to donkeys, badgers to sheep, even eagles and bears had their place in camp and on the battlefield. Some American Civil War mascots were an inspiration for the troops, while others acted as a reminder of beloved pets at home. Mascots brought loyalty and enthusiasm, and for soldiers, the act of nurturing animals also offset boredom in camp.

Documented mascots include General Robert E. Lee's pet hen, who rewarded him with an egg laid under his cot each morning for his breakfast. The hen was misplaced during the Battle of Gettysburg in the summer of 1863, causing much consternation until she was found. The 3rd Louisiana CSA had

2 See 'The Knowledge: Remembering our fallen comrades', The Times, 8–14 July 2006, pp. 30–3

3 http://www.thisislocallondon.co.uk/display.var.852833.0.meet_jake_the_77_hero_dog.php

a donkey who would push into the commander's tent and try to sleep with him, mistaking the officer for his original owner!

The 12th Wisconsin Volunteers had a tame bear who marched with them all the way to Missouri and the 2nd Rhode Islanders kept a sheep named Dick, who was taught tricks by the men. Soldiers of the Richmond Howitzers kept a number of gamecocks as pets. This battalion also had a dog, Stonewall, who was much admired by the artillerymen. Stonewall was given rides in the safety of a limber chest during battle. He was taught to attend roll call, sitting on his haunches in line. The 26th Wisconsin Volunteer Infantry had a badger as a mascot (the Badger State) and both the 12th Wisconsin and the 104th Pennsylvania kept tame raccoons as unit mascots.[4]

NORTHERN IRELAND

Rats, a brown-and-white little mongrel, was known as the Soldier Dog of Ulster. His active service days were spent in Crossmaglen in Northern Ireland. He spent his duty time in the front line and was injured more than once. Rats was blown up, run over and shot at many times, but was welcome company when the troops had to go out on a mission and he became a trusted 'nose' for potential danger. He went with them on day and night manoeuvres, flew in helicopter missions and was no stranger to front-line action.

He suffered a broken leg, gunshot injuries and shrapnel in his spine, among other injuries. On top of that, Rats made

4 http://oha.ci.alexandria.va.us/fortward/special-sections/ mascots/#2

enemies among IRA supporters as he was the troops' mascot and helped boost morale when it was most needed. This made him a potential IRA target.

Rats became well known among the serving soldiers. There were many times when he warned a patrol that something was amiss and as a result he saved a few lives. A BBC documentary on him told of his devotion to the troops and a book written by Max Halstock tells of the courage and bravery of this little dog. It also points out that Rats went through many difficult times in his life when the regiments changed over once their tour of duty was over. This meant that he lost the men to whom he had become attached more than once; something the little dog could never understand. There must have been times when he was very sad and confused.

Rats was held in such high esteem by the troops that he was given an army number. This was put on a medal made from a dog disc. It had the Queen's head on one side and 'Rats. Delta 777' on the other. Rats received the medal during a ceremony when the whole company was on parade and a piper played 'Scotland the Brave' in his honour.

Rats had developed a close relationship with Corporal O'Neil of the Queen's Own Highlanders. He looked after him, but his tour of duty came to an end and Corporal O'Neil had to leave Crossmaglen. The regiment that replaced the Queen's Own Highlanders was the Prince of Wales Company, 1st Battalion, Welsh Guards. All the comrades that he had grown close to were going to leave. Corporal O'Neil was not allowed to take Rats home with him and it was a sad parting for them both. Rats had to find new friends among the new soldiers and, in time, he became close to Corporal Lewis of the Welsh Guards.

Rats continued his tour of duty, being a mascot and a great morale booster for the troops. Later, he was retired to a secret location in the UK. Secret because the army wanted to be sure that the IRA did not target Rats in an attempt to demoralise the men. He had meant so much to them and had been a welcome diversion and help through such difficult times. Rats had a happy retirement and still holds a special place in the soldiers' memories of duty in Northern Ireland.[5]

A lovely account in Juliet Gardiner's latest book *The Animal's War*, which accompanies the Imperial War Museum exhibition, involved Sergeant Christopher Batta, the handler of a Belgian Malinois sniffer dog called Carlo. On a sixty-day tour of Kuwait, Carlo discovered a phenomenal 167 caches of explosives. Returning to America, Sergeant Batta was awarded a Bronze Star, but on learning that there was no award for Carlo, he whipped off his medal and hung it round Carlo's neck, saying that he worked harder and was always in front![6]

There are also countless other tales, such as that of Winkie, a pigeon, who saved the lives of an air crew ditched at sea by carrying home details of their position. Thrown free of her onboard container, the bird flew an incredible 120 miles from the site of the crashed Beaufort bomber to deliver an SOS to the Scottish coast.

5 http://homepage.ntlworld.com/k.westgate/history.htm
6 Gardiner, J., *The Animal's War*, Portrait, London 2006

THE ONGOING WAR ON TERRORISM

Not enough can be said about the heroic individuals, both bipeds and quadrupeds, who have loaned their abilities to the security and rescue efforts in the wake of the terrorist attacks on America and the UK. Since security has been stepped up at our airports and seaports, human and canine teams expedite inspections at borders. They work tirelessly to combat terrorist threats, as well as to stopping the flow of illegal narcotics and detect unreported currency, concealed humans, bombs, guns and smuggled agriculture products.

WORLD TRADE CENTER, SEPTEMBER 11 2001

When one thinks of animals at war we are mistaken to look back to the black-and-white images of the early and mid-1900s alone. Animals are still used today to aid mankind in the present war on terror.

Police K9 Sirius, Badge Number 17, a four-and-a-half-year-old, 90-lb, easy-going, yellow Labrador-Retriever was an Explosive Detection Dog with the Port Authority of New York and New Jersey Police Department. Sirius, along with his partner, Police Officer David Lim, was assigned to the World Trade Center in New York, where their primary duty was to check vehicles entering the complex, clear unattended bags and sweep areas for VIP safety. Sirius, who began work at the World Trade Center on 4 July 2000, was the only police dog to perish during the attack on the Twin Towers.

On the morning of September 11 2001, Sirius and Officer Lim were at their station which was located in the basement of Tower Two. When Officer Lim heard the explosion, he thought at first that a bomb had been detonated inside the building. Believing he would be more effective alone, he left Sirius locked in his 6-by-10-feet crate, telling him, 'I'll be back to get you,' as he rushed to help with the rescue effort. At that time, Officer Lim could think of no safer place for his canine companion other than the basement. However, he failed to return to Sirius. Becoming trapped in the falling debris of Tower One, he wasn't rescued until some five hours or more later. Sadly, in the meantime, Sirius had perished when Tower Two collapsed. The remains of the loyal dog were recovered on 22 January 2002. Thankfully, it is believed he died instantly when his kennel caved in.

Sirius, who born in 1997, was given full police honours when his body was eventually retrieved from the rubble that was Ground Zero. The huge machines on the site were silenced, and he was saluted by all in attendance as Officer Lim carried the remains of his flag-draped partner to a waiting police truck. The American flag which had covered the dog's body was later given to Officer Lim and a Fifth Grade Class in Illinois purchased an oak memorial flag box for its safekeeping. Sirius was cremated and his ashes placed in an oaken urn which Officer Lim keeps at his home until a decision can be made as to where he will finally be interred.

A memorial service for Sirius was held on 24 April 2002 at Liberty State Park (North Field) in Jersey City, New Jersey. Earlier that month, he had been posthumously awarded the Victoria Cross at the British Embassy in Manhattan. Almost 100 police dogs, many wearing badges covered by black ribbon to match those of their handlers, and some from as far away as California, filed past the wooden urn containing the ashes of Sirius, as their handlers stopped to salute. A trumpeter sounded 'Taps', bagpipers played 'Amazing Grace' and seven officers fired a twenty-one-gun salute. An oil painting of Sirius entitled 'Salute to Sirius', painted by Debbie Miller Stonebraker and privately commissioned by Sandee Nastasi of Long Island as a gift to the NY/NY Port Authority Police Department K-9 Unit, was unveiled and a poem read in his honour. Officer Lim, who had been Sirius' handler for two and a half years, was then presented with his companion's stainless steel water bowl engraved with a tribute to the brave dog.

For some time, it was feared that the body of Sirius might never be recovered from the tons of debris, but, at last, Officer Lim was able to make good on the final words given to his staunch companion on that morning of September 11 2001 and comfort must be taken when and where it can.[7]

LONDON, 7 JULY 2005

In 2005 after the London Bombings, a Springer Spaniel called Richie was sent onto the Tavistock Square bus (and into the surrounding area) to check for secondary devices. The bombed trains were also checked over by dogs who were immediately on the scene.

Another young hero of the day was the cocker spaniel Jake, who saved the lives of several badly wounded victims on the bombed bus in Tavistock Square. Just two months after his police

7 http://www.novareinna.com/bridge/sirius.html

115

training, the little dog and his handler, PC Robert Crawford, cleared a way through the wreckage for explosives officers to reach a suspected second bomb – a microwave box on the parcel rack behind the driver. Once it was made safe, paramedics could treat the injured. 'It was quite horrific,' remembers PC Crawford. 'But Jake seemed to take it in his stride.'[8]

One Guide Dog who led his owner to safety in the immediate aftermath of the central London Bombings on 7 July, was Tom. Mike Townsend, a Guide Dogs' trustee and blind since birth, was down in London for a meeting and had just left his hotel room. As he stood at a crossing, Tom tugged at him to get him across. He hurried up the street and was about 150 yards away when the bomb went off on the Number 30 bus.

Mike said, 'All sorts of thoughts rushed through my mind. What if there was another bomb, and would I never see my wife and daughter again?' He said he could feel people rushing past as a sense of panic took over the scene, and then it became eerily quiet because the police had closed off many streets. Later he found out that a minute after he left his hotel, the concierge was standing at the crossing helping a lady with her bags and she died instantly when the bus exploded. 'I really couldn't say if Tom knew something was going to happen,'[9] Mike said.

> 'We started to make our way as best we could and to be honest it felt as though Tom did not know where he was going. At one point I got quite upset with him when he

8 http://www.thisislocallondon.co.uk/display.var.852833.0.meet_jake_the_77_hero_dog.php

9 Adapted from www.people.co.uk/petsandpeople/tm_objectid=15916354&method=m2_columnist_nav_archive-name_page.html

started taking us down a route neither of us was familiar with. But it says something about Tom's training that I can honestly say he was not fazed at all. Every time we came up to a road block he would turn away and find an alternative route. His confidence was inspiring and, amazingly, he not only got me safely to my meeting, but we arrived on time.'[(10)]

THE DICKIN MEDAL

In 1942 the People's Dispensary For Sick Animals (PDSA) founder, Maria Dickin, came up with the idea of introducing a medal to honour animals who had served with the Armed Forces and the Civil Defence units during World War II.

To date, pigeons, horses, cats and dogs had received the award. The Dickin Medal is considered to be the Victoria Cross for animals and is given to any animal who displays conspicuous gallantry and devotion to duty, associated with or under control of any branch of the Armed Forces or Civil Defence units. It will only be awarded on recommendation and is exclusive to the animal kingdom. The medal is made of bronze. At the top are the letters 'PDSA', and in the middle is written 'FOR GALLANTRY'. Underneath that is written, 'WE ALSO SERVE'.

The first dog to receive the Dickin Medal was Bob, a white mongrel. Attached to an infantry unit, he, like the soldiers was sent out on a mission. Suddenly, Bob froze and he could not be

10 Adapted from http://www.guidedogs.org.uk

moved. A sudden noise betrayed the enemy presence and because of Bob the men were not killed or captured.

Simon is the only cat to have received the award after being the rat-catcher aboard HMS *Amethyst* when she was attacked on the Yangtze River by Chinese communists in 1949. The black-and-white cat was hit by shrapnel and badly singed when the ship was shelled on 20 April 1949, but she continued to get rid of rats and helped boost morale while the ship was trapped on the river. HMS *Amethyst* eventually escaped communist guns by making a risky night-time retreat.

Simon, whose citation for the Dickin Medal was reported in *The Times* on 5 August 1949, became such a popular figure among the public that the captain appointed Stewart Hett as Cat Officer to cope with all the resulting fan mail. Lieutenant-Commander Hett, now almost eighty, said that Simon inspired the nation to write letters of support. 'He received between 150 and 180 letters. Some sent bits of fish. Some sent collars'!

The Dickin Medal was also awarded to Antis, an Alsatian, on 28 January 1949. Antis served with his Czech owner in the French Air Force and the RAF from 1940 to 1945 in both North Africa and England. He was the first foreign dog to receive the Dickin Medal.

Sheila, a Sheepdog, was awarded the Dickin Medal on 2 July 1945 in Scotland 'for assisting the rescue of four American Airmen lost in a blizzard after an air crash in December 1944'. She was the first civilian dog to be awarded the Dickin Medal.

More recently, Britain's top dog in Iraq was Buster, a six-year-old Springer Spaniel with the Duke of Wellington Regiment. In 2003, he was used to sniff out the supply of insurgent arms and ammunition which several human searches had failed to find. Buster was the sixtieth animal in the sixtieth year to receive the Dicken Medal, which was won some 40 years earlier by Winkie the pigeon.[11]

Even the sixtieth anniversary of the D-Day celebrations in 2004 rightly honoured the valour of human veterans, but no one mentioned Bing the Alsatian, who was dropped into Normandy on D-Day with the 13th Battalion Parachute Regiment and landed in a tree, where he remained all night through the enemy shelling. Although badly wounded in the neck and eyes, once he was cut free of his parachute, Bing stood guard on a vital section of the battalion's front, his presence a huge comfort to the troops, especially at night.

There was also Rob the paradog, who made two drops and was also awarded the Dicken Medal for leading SAS patrols into enemy territory. Rob even made it home after the war and settled happily into farm life!

Other dogs who received the medal include:

- Jet, who served with the Civil Defence. Awarded the Dickin Medal on 12 January 1945 'for being responsible for the rescue of persons trapped under blitzed buildings while serving with the Civil Defence Service in London'.

- Irma, who served with the Civil Defence. Awarded the Dickin Medal on 12 January 1945 'for being responsible for the rescue of trapped persons under blitzed buildings while serving with the Civil Defence Service in London'.

11 'The Knowledge: Remembering our fallen comrades', *The Times*, 8–14 July 2006, pp. 30–3

- Rob (War Dog) No. 471/322, Special Air Service. Awarded the Dickin Medal on 22 January 1945 'for taking part in landings during the North African campaign with Infantry and later with the Special Air Unit in Italy'.

- Thorn, who served with the Civil Defence. Awarded the Dickin Medal on 2 March 1945 'for locating air raid casualties, in spite of thick smoke in burning buildings'.

- Tich, a mongrel bitch. Awarded the Dickin Medal on 1 July 1949 'for loyalty, courage and devotion to duty under hazardous conditions of war from 1941 to 1945, while serving in North Africa and Italy'.

- Gander, a Newfoundland. Awarded the Dickin Medal on 15 August 2000. Gander was the first dog for fifty-five years to be awarded the Dickin Medal and the only dog from Canada. The citation reads, 'For saving lives of Canadian infantrymen during the battle of Lye Mun on Hong Kong Island in December 1941'.

- Rifleman Khan dog, 147, 6th Battalion meronians. Awarded the Dickin Medal on 27 March 1945 'for rescuing L/Cpl Muldoon from drowning while under heavy shell fire at the battle of Walcheren, November 1944'.

- Rex, rescue dog of the Civil Defence. Awarded the Dickin Medal in April 1945 'for outstanding good work in the location of casualties in burning buildings. Undaunted by smouldering debris, thick smoke, intense heat and jets of water from fire hoses, this dog displayed uncanny intelligence and outstanding determination in his efforts to follow up a scent that led him to a casualty'.

- Rip, a mongrel dog, who, was picked up by the Civil Defence Squad in London E14. Awarded the Dickin Medal 'for locating many air raid victims buried by rubble during the blitz of 1940'.

- Peter, a Collie dog. Awarded the Dickin Medal in November 1946 'for locating victims trapped under blitzed buildings while serving with the Civil Defence Units'.

- Punch and Judy, a Boxer dog and bitch. Awarded the Dickin Medal in November 1946: 'these dogs saved the lives of two British Officers in Israel by attacking an armed terrorist who was stealing upon them unawares and thus warning them of the danger – Punch sustained bullet wounds and Judy received a graze down her back'.

- Ricky, a Welsh Sheepdog. Awarded the Dickin Medal on 29 March 1947: 'this dog was engaged in clearing the verges of a canal bank in Holland. He found all mines but during the operation one of them exploded. Ricky was wounded but remained calm and kept on working. Had he become excited, he would have endangered the rest of the section working nearby'.

• Brian, an Alsatian. Awarded the Dickin Medal on 29 March 1947: 'this patrol dog was attached to a Parachute Battalion. He landed in Normandy and, after doing the required number of jumps, became a fully qualified Paratrooper'.[12]

On September 11 2001, the world at large saw a tragedy unfold. I am sure we can all recall where we were when news broke of the twin towers of the World Trade Center collapsing after a terrorist attack. Over 300 dogs were brought into the site we now know as Ground Zero. The New York Police Department (NYPD) dogs were the first there. Appollo, part of the NYPD K9 Search and Rescue Team, was on the scene within just fifteen minutes of the disaster.

Two Guide Dogs who saved their owners' lives just before the World Trade Center collapsed have been honoured for their bravery. Riva and Salty made their way down from the seventy-first floor. They guided their blind owners, Mr Hingson and Mr Roselle, through crowded, smoke-filled stairs. They also managed to lead another woman to safety.

On 5 March 2002, the Chairman of the PDSA presented Appollo, Riva and Salty with Dickin Medals, 'For their service to humanity'.

12 List taken from http://homepage.ntlworld.com/k.westgate/history5.htm

One of the few good things about exploration and war was the bond and love that developed between soldiers and their animals. For a man away from the comfort and security of home, missing his wife and family and literally facing death, a horse, ox, or ferret mascot that could return affection was an immeasurable comfort. These creatures were also of huge significance to those feeling isolated in high command. Like President Bush today, General Eisenhower adored cheerful black 'Scottie' dogs. His own dog accompanied him everywhere on campaigns and was, he claimed, 'the only living thing he could talk to who didn't want to discuss the war'. Juliet Gardiner's research also revealed Winston Churchill's passion for animals, including a gold-and-blue parrot which he taught to say 'F*** the Nazis'!

And dogs go way beyond helping out during wartime. In 1991, after twenty years in the Royal Navy, Chief Petty Officer Allen Parton suffered severe head trauma in a road accident during the Gulf War. He was, he recalls, 'a blob in a wheelchair' who could not speak, write or walk. The once happily married man had lost his ability to love, laugh or cry, along with the memories of his wedding to nurse Sandra as well as the birth of their two young children, Liam and Zoe. 'We sort of plodded on as a family, but I didn't love them. I was a completely different person,' he recalled.

Nine years ago Parton accompanied his wife to a class where she served as puppy walker for Canine Partners – a charity training dogs to help disabled people. Endal, a little yellow Labrador with a health and attitude problem, instinctively started to pile objects into Parton's lap, eliciting his first smile in half a decade. 'It seems two crocks together made a dream team,' he says.

Endal understands over 1,000 commands in sign language. 'Though I couldn't talk to humans, I could communicate with a dog. He also gave me back the emotions I have lost.' The dog can even operate a chip-and-pin machine, load the washing machine and lift the toilet seat for Parton. ('Being a man-dog, he won't put it down.') In 2002 the Labrador was Parton's best man when he re-married Sandra. The Partons' marriage was one of just five in eighty-five that survived the husband being injured in the Gulf War.

'I was a serviceman who had lost the will to live,' said Parton. 'I've had two attempts at suicide. I had lost my past, I had lost my future. Now I'm back with my wife and children because of a dog.'

In 2001, Endal saved Parton's life when a speeding car knocked him out of his wheelchair. He put his owner in the recovery position, covered him with a blanket, fetched his mobile phone and sought help. For that, the dog was awarded the PDSA gold medal for peacetime bravery.[13]

DOGS, RATS AND LANDMINES

We all realise that much goes on within the government that we do not know, and perhaps in some cases, will never know. Interestingly, back in 1953, the US Army commissioned a report by Dr Joseph Banks Rhine, who was based at Duke University and was the foremost researcher in the field of parapsychology

13 Taken from http://www.thisislocallondon.co.uk/display.var.852833.0.meet_jake_the_77_hero_dog.php and 'My Dog Saved my Life', *Independent on Sunday*, 5 March 2006, p. 54

(or, using the term he coined: extrasensory perception). The purpose of his report was to research the possibility of using dogs and other animals to detect buried landmines under conditions that gave no normal sensory cues. Conclusions were considered so sensitive that they remained classified until recently. The final report (dated 10 July 1953) remained classified as 'confidential' for more than fifty years, until it was recently declassified after a long, laborious process. It took ten separate offices five years to clear this short report for release.

This final report, entitled 'Final Report for Contract DA-44-009-ENG-1039', codename 'Animal E.S.P.', describes a series of experiments involving German Shepherds trying to locate buried landmines. The results appeared promising but also suggested that at least some of the positive results were attributable to the dogs' remarkable sense of smell. Not only this, the report also examines the possibility of ESP in cats and pigeons.

Dr Rhine was the first to attempt a scientific investigation of paranormal phenomena of this type. According to him, 'an investigation of the available reports, and visits to England to learn what the British Army had found, led to a serious question as to whether the claim was well founded'. His experiments focused on German Schu mines buried in a few inches of moist sand. A tough nut to crack, you will agree. Only two years and fifteen gruelling typed pages later, Dr Rhine concluded that 'dogs can be trained to locate mines... and there can be no doubt but that, for the most part, this is a sensory function, olfactory in type'.

However, dogs were used but had their drawbacks. For one thing, their weight was enough to set off a mine. It also took a lot of training and many dogs needed to be used, which of course was a huge expense. To combat this, another animal has been brought into the fore: the humble rat.

In November 2003, a Belgian research project for detecting landmines using specially trained sniffer rats was launched when the first batch of rodents was sent on its initial assignment to Mozambique. African giant pouched rats were trained over three years to sniff out explosives at a test site in Tanzania. They spent two months in field trials among heavily mined areas of Mozambique, along the banks of the Limpopo. Landmines are an insidious legacy of the conflict that maims and kills Mozambicans to this day, including rural children born long after the guns were silenced.

Scientists involved in the project said that in many ways rats were better mine-hunters than dogs as they learn quicker and do not get so personally attached to the owner, so they are easier to transfer to another trainer. Researchers also said rats, being lightweight, were easier to transport and less likely to accidentally set off mines. Bartes Weetjens, who first thought of the idea eight years ago after recalling that the rodents he bred as a childhood hobby had an acute sense of smell, said that rats' noses are closer to the ground, so they can operate in an area of high mine density, where a dog may be confused.

In 2005, the Belgian de-mining research group APOPO had eight rodents working alongside dogs and metal detectors on a minefield in Mozambique's coastal town of Vilanculos, some 650 kilometres north-east of the capital Maputo. The Gambian giant pouched rats helped to clear a stretch of fertile land that has lain fallow since a savage civil war ended in 1992. 'The biggest problem in landmines is that from the moment there is a mine somewhere, a very large area becomes suspect and has to be cleared before people can go back to farming there,' said Frank Weetjens, APOPO's representative in Mozambique.

The rats there are considered the latest weapon in the war to remove more than 100 million landmines scattered in some sixty countries that kill or injure an estimated fifty people daily. Leaders of 143 countries met in 2004 to plan the next steps in their global campaign.

The choice of this breed of rat is very thorough – of course it has to stand the temperatures and habitat of Africa and this rat's home range is found throughout much of Africa. It gets its name from the large pouches on the inside of its cheeks, which it uses for carrying food. Easily tamed, the rodent is a favourite in the pet trade.

The methods currently used in mine clearance have drawbacks. Metal detectors are very slow and tedious because they pick up every single metal fragment in a suspected minefield, be it garbage or an actual mine, which of course is time consuming. After World War II, dogs emerged as the most reliable detection method, able to sniff out even those mines buried 15–20 cm below ground, which a metal detector will miss. Growing to a maximum weight of 2.8 kg, a dog can scamper round a minefield without the risk of detonating anti-personnel gadgets that can be triggered by its heavier canine colleague.

The rats are attached to little red harnesses and guided down the length of a 100-sq m field by their trainer. When the rat hits on a suspected mine, it stops, sniffs and starts to scratch at the ground, and is then rewarded with a piece of banana.

To most rural Africans, rats are either a pest or added protein for an evening meal so it took a while for them to be accepted! But in a country where the problem of landmines has been an obstacle to attempts to re-build an economy ravaged by sixteen years of civil war, every single battle plan counts for something. 'The rat is another tool. It's new for us but it is going to be a very important tool in de-mining,' said Jacky D'Almeida, director of the Accelerated De-mining Program (ADP), an organisation working with APOPO in Vilanculos, which relies mainly on metal detectors and dogs. 'Every tool has its own limitations. Machines, dogs, men have limitations, and so do the rats. What is important is that we have a package that can speed up the process and we can reduce costs and increase productivity.' And for Mozambique, rated one of the world's poorest countries, cost-saving is vital.

Inspired by this, the Columbian government has followed suit. Colombia was in fact home to the world's highest number of mine-related deaths and injuries in 2006. According to the government, more than 1,075 Colombians were killed or maimed when they stepped onto mines in 2005 – a higher number than in any other heavily mined country such as Cambodia or Afghanistan.

Six rats, including 'Lola', are currently being trained by the government to sniff out explosive devices planted by leftist rebels. Lola has a 90 per cent success rate in locating explosive material in her laboratory training maze. Police animal trainers, tired of seeing their explosive-sniffing dogs blown up, hope the white-furred, pink-eyed creature will lead her classmates through upcoming open field tests and then into the Andean country's live minefields before the end of 2006.

At about 220g, Lola is too light to detonate landmines that guerrillas set to protect crops used to make cocaine, which they sell to fund their revolution of four decades. It takes about 400g of pressure to detonate a mine. Security experts say they expect the Revolutionary Armed Forces of Colombia (FARC) and the smaller National Liberation Army (ELN) to keep planting mines because they are effective in preventing soldiers and police from encroaching on their coca fields and the camps they use to hold thousands of kidnapping victims.

About 60 per cent of Colombia's victims of exploding mines are members of state security forces. The remaining 40 per cent are civilians, about half of them children, who step on the devices while walking to school or playing in the countryside. According to the government there are minefields on the outskirts of most Colombian towns, littered with a total of more than 100,000 of the devices.

Police animal trainer Jose Pineda states that rats have more sensitive noses than dogs, which should allow them to sniff out mines in difficult terrain better. Plus, they are cheaper than dogs, eat less, are easier to transport and can wriggle into smaller spaces while hunting.

Little is documented about the animals that helped us through the wars. In fact, the only thing we in Britain have as a lasting reminder of is the monument recently erected as a result of the Animals in War Memorial Fund founded by Jilly Cooper and a group of her friends, who include Joanna Lumley, Kate Adie and General Peter Davies, former head of the RSCPA. The monument was unveiled in Park Lane in November 2004 with the words 'They had no choice' inscribed on it. As Jilly herself said, 'They had no idea why they were fighting or when the nightmare would end. They gave their service, their lives and their love without any thought of reward.'[14]

SNIFFER BEES

In May 2006 the *Independent on Sunday* reported that a British company has developed a device to detect explosives at airports with the help of specially trained honey bees.[15] In remarkable field trials, scientists have harnessed the insects' powerful sense of smell to track down samples of TNT, Semtex, gunpowder and other explosives hidden in shipments passing through a busy cargo airport.

The project is the result of five years of Government-funded research carried out by scientists from Rothamsted Research Centre in Hertfordshire with the prototype under trial consisting of a shoebox-sized device nicknamed the 'buzz box', containing three trained bees harnessed into a removable drawer. An electric fan draws air into the box, while a video camera records the bees' response, which can alert the handler to even the faintest trace of explosives.

According to the researchers, bees are able to detect the scent of explosives at concentrations as low as two parts per trillion. 'It's the equivalent of finding a grain of sand in a swimming pool,' said Rachael Carson, general manager of Inscentinel, the company behind the research. 'If you give them the smell, and

14 Quote from *The Times* Knowledge 8–14 July 2006, p.33
15 'Sniffer Bees' by Martin Hodgson, *Independent on Sunday*, 7 May 2006, p.14

then reward them with a sugar solution, they quickly make the association between the smell and the food.'

After training, bees will react to the smallest trace of an explosive by extending their tongue-like proboscis in anticipation of food. 'It's like Pavlov's dogs salivating at the sound of a bell,' Ms Carson added. Unlike dogs, however, bees are quick to learn and relatively cheap to maintain. Furthermore, they do not need a dedicated handler and cannot be distracted from their task.

Inscentinel now hopes to produce a commercially available bee-powered bomb detector within two years. According to Ms Carson, the 'buzz box' could also be used to search for drugs and contraband tobacco, but Inscentinel is also exploring various non-security related applications. The device could, for instance, be used to monitor food quality, or even to detect changes in blood or urine caused by illness. A separate trial has been launched in conjunction with the London School of Tropical Medicine into the possibility of detecting signs of tuberculosis in a patient's breath, Ms Carson said.

Richard Jones, director of the International Bee Research Association, said that although bees can be trained, the experience of being strapped in a box could well distort their reactions. 'Any animal under stress will behave differently. I think you'd be better off with a Spaniel,' he commented.

There is another potential sting in the tail, too: certain natural compounds would cause any bee to react, even if it had received counter-explosives training. 'That could be a problem if someone was carrying lots of honey,' said Inscentinel director Stephen James.

We must remember, however, that for each story we know of, and rejoice about, there are still many unsung animal heroes in the world who deserve our gratitude and respect, and who will never get the recognition that they deserve.

CHAPTER 7

Animals as Therapy

'There is no psychiatrist in the world like a puppy licking your face.'

BEN WILLIAMS

Pets are known to have a calming influence but now their healing properties have been acknowledged by doctors and they can work miracles for children in hospital. For some people, the idea of a wagging tail or wet nose around an ill or frail person may seem terribly unorthodox, but increasing research highlights there is a special place for animals in treating the sick and terminally ill. Often they help where human therapists have failed. Animals can act as a breath of fresh air, brightening up the days of patients or housebound people. Patients can share their fears, have an unconditional hug or confide secrets they wouldn't share with anyone else.

Given the right animal, people and circumstances, pets can indeed serve as 'therapists'. In Britain and many other countries, animals are routinely taken into hospitals, nursing and care homes, schools and community centres. For the visit to be safe and effective, the animal must be carefully assessed and the pet's owner trained to guide the animal-human interaction. Even in less formal, animal-assisted activities, where the animal is introduced to an individual or group with no specific therapeutic goal, patients and staff often experience improved morale and communication.

Research states that patients in hospitals and nursing homes who have regular visits from pets – whether their own or those brought in from organisations – are more receptive to medical treatment and nourishment. Animals give the patient the will to live and, in nursing homes, medical staff are often surprised to see residents suddenly 'come alive'. Animals simply have a calming effect on humans and benefit mental wellbeing, especially in children and the elderly.

Things have taken a dramatic leap in the last few years with pet therapy becoming far more acceptable as a valuable aid in reaching out to the elderly, the infirm and to ill or abused children throughout the country. Therapy Animals pay visits to mainstream schools, special schools, convalescent homes, hospitals, hospices, day-care centres, residential homes and prisons. They can be both pedigree and mixed breed. In fact, Therapy Animals come in all shapes and sizes. Cats and small dogs are good because they can be lifted easily and fit on even the smallest laps. Alternatively, larger dogs are just as useful as a companion for the elderly or disabled person confined to their bed or chairs, as they are just the right height to sit patiently next to them, allowing the occupant to stroke their fur.

The one underlying commonality is that all Therapy Cats and Dogs have a calm, gentle personality and are people-oriented. They must love attention and petting, and not be at all shy. In addition, they need basic obedience training and should be conditioned to sudden noises, such as a falling crutch or hospital beeps and machinery.

It has also been found that children, especially those who are abused or neglected, are able to communicate with animals far more easily than they can with an adult. A pet offers a safe place for a child with emotional problems: It gives unconditional love, providing a security blanket.

ANIMAL THERAPY

Astonishingly, Animal Therapy has been recorded since the ninth century, when doctors in Flanders encouraged disabled patients to look after animals to 're-establish the harmony of soul and body'. Today, there is growing evidence that contact with animals can speed recovery times and combat depression. Research at the University of Zagreb revealed that Croatian children caught up in the Balkans conflict were more able to deal with the traumatic experiences they had witnessed if they owned a pet.

Animals are reputed to help Alzheimers' patients who often exist in a world of their own. Having an animal around can bring them back to the present moment. Specially trained puppies can also alert others when an Alzheimers' patient wanders into harm's way. 'Pets can provide a measure of safety to people with the disease,' says Thomas Kirk, vice president of a chapter of the Alzheimers' Association.

It has also been cited that pets can aid children who suffer from Attention Deficit Disorder (ADD), as they are able to focus on a pet, which helps them learn to concentrate. Mentally ill patients, or those with emotional problems, share a common bond when a cat or dog enters the room. Instead of reacting negatively to one another, the animal boosts morale and fosters a positive environment.

Everyday pet animals have also been found to have psychological benefits in people suffering from serious illness. For example, a study of AIDS patients conducted by Siegal[1] in 1999 found that pets provide a level of companionship that helped patients cope with the stress of their illness. The study looked at more than 1,800 patients and found that those who did not have a pet were more than twice as likely to report symptoms of depression. In addition to tactile comfort, pets may provide a relationship that, unlike many human relationships, is unaffected by the presence of a serious illness.

Straede and Gates[2] investigated the psychological health benefits of owning cats. In the study, ninety-two cat owners (aged 12–74 years) and seventy non-pet owners (aged 19–64 years) were surveyed to determine the relationship between psychological health and pet ownership. Findings showed that cat owners had significantly lower scores for general psychological health, indicating a lower level of psychiatric

1 Siegal, J., *Journal of AIDS Care*, 1999

2 Straede, C.M. and Gates, R.G., 'Psychological health in a population of Australian cat owners', *Anthrozoos*, Vol. 6, pp. 30–42, 1993

disturbance, and could be considered to have better psychological health than the non-pet owners.

Mischel[3] carried out a study, which looked at the therapeutic effects of pets on patients with terminal cancer. Four to six volunteers brought kittens, cats, puppies and dogs to a nursing facility to visit fifteen terminally-ill cancer patients. All medical interventions for participants had ceased. Participants were administered a six-item, cleverly-worded questionnaire and then, during two animal visits, they were asked two more non-directive questions. Results showed that contact with the animals reduced feelings of anxiety and despair and helped the participants to move more easily through the stages of death. Animals were thought to have facilitated the relinquishing of past relationships by being with participants, emotionally and physically. It was also found that participants who evidenced more warmth, humour, creativity, capacity for enjoyment and empathy benefited most from therapeutic visits. This research was also supported in a recent study by Millhouse-Flourie[4] who found that the use of therapeutic visits was successful in mitochondrial disease. It was found that patients reported a greater sense of wellbeing following such visits.

Wolff and Frishman[5] researched the use of animal assisted therapy in cardiovascular disease. They found that the presence of a Therapy Dog led to participants reporting a

3 Mischel, I. J. (1984). Pets As Therapy visits with terminal cancer patients. Social-casework No. 65, pp. 451–458

4 Millhouse-Flourie, T. J., 'Physical, occupational, respiratory, speech, equine and pet therapies for mitochondrial disease', *Mitochondrian* 4 (5–6), pp. 549–58, 2004

5 Wolff, A.I. and Frishman, W.H., Animal assisted therapy in cardiovascular disease, *Journal of Psychosomatic Research*, Vol. 49 (4), pp. 275–80, 2000

better quality of life. Participants who saw a Therapy Dog were also more likely to survive for a longer period of time.

Some studies have also looked at the short-term benefits of the presence of animals and this is where things get interesting and open up a world of opportunity for non-pet owners benefiting from their presence. For example, the elderly living in residential homes where pets are not allowed, or patients recovering in hospital or terminally-ill people in hospital – even children in schools – the list is endless. Any animal lover can witness the benefits of owning a pet from being in their presence for just a short while. For example, researchers Anderson, Reid and Jennings subjected participants to stressful mental arithmetic tasks with pets, a close friend, or neither present. Measures of skin conductance (in which the function of sweat glands is assessed), blood pressure and pulse rate were recorded. Those patients who took the tests in the presence of a pet had lower blood pressure and pulse rates than the ones without a pet, a friend or neither accompanying them.

Freidman, Katcher and Thomas also found that being in the presence of a dog, or petting an animal, can reduce blood pressure. Watson and Weinstein also discovered that a test for fear, worry and stress in a person, the Spielbergers State Anxiety Score, to be significantly lower in participants who were petting a dog compared to those in a controlled condition with no dog present.

Across the UK, colleges and universities are constantly designing professional-level qualifications in the new and expanding area of using animals not only on a companion basis, but also within the medical and psychological profession as therapy.

VISITING THERAPY ANIMALS

'All over the world, major universities researching the therapeutic value of pets in our society and the number of hospitals, nursing homes, prisons and mental institutions are employing full-time pet therapists.'

BETTY WHITE, AMERICAN ACTRESS, ANIMAL
ACTIVIST AND AUTHOR OF PET LOVE

One of the first people to describe the potential of nursing home pets was Boris Levinson.[1] He pointed out the need for the elderly to have someone to love. Levinson suggested pets could restore a sense of identity and serve as a love object, which the patient can hug and kiss. Bustad (1980, cited in Katcher and Beck 1983) suggested pets have a hugely positive effect on the elderly. They provide a more secure grasp of reality and restore order to their lives. Corson, (1981, cited in Katcher and Beck 1983) also suggested companion animals could act as bonding catalysts in geriatric institutions.

H.M. Hendy (1987) carried out a study which looked at the effects of pets' and/or people's visits on nursing-home residents. He found that there were no significant benefits of the pet-alone condition over the people-plus-pet or people-alone conditions of the experiment. The experimented suggested that further research was required to examine the characteristics that make effective pet visits to nursing homes. However other research in nursing homes has found benefits of visiting pets.

1 Levinson, 1970, cited in Katcher, A.H. and Beck, A.M., *New Perspectives on Our Lives with Companion Animals*, University of Pennsylvania Press, 1983

Robinson, Fenwick and Blackshaw (1999) looked at the benefits of resident dogs and visiting dogs in nursing homes. The study considered the long-term benefits of the dogs. It was found that the resident dog reduced tension and confusion, as well as depression and fatigue. The visiting dog's presence helped decrease levels of fatigue, too. Researchers concluded the most beneficial effects were seen with the resident dog. However, they also stated that a visiting dog might be beneficial, too, especially if a resident dog is not an option.

A more recent study by Columbo et al (2006) looked at the benefits of therapeutic visits on the institutionalised elderly in Italy. Participants were given either a plant, a canary, or nothing. They were observed for a period of three months and following this, it was found that the participants with the canary reported less depressive symptoms and a better quality of life than either of the other groups.

Cass[2] suggested some very specific conditions and circumstances are required for the successful use of pet-facilitated therapy. He emphasises that the animals in the institutions do not offer a potential threat to health and also suggests rules for the sanitation and maintenance of the pets, while, for the elderly, small, sedate dogs with quiet temperaments should be chosen.

Levinson[3] suggests that it is isolated and socially unresponsive individuals who stand to benefit most from the companionship of animals. This also suggests that companion animals somehow have the capacity to reconnect such people

2 Cass, 1981, cited in Katcher, A.H. and Beck, A.M., New Perspectives on Our Lives with Companion Animals, University of Pennsylvania Press, 1983

3 Levison, 1980, cited in Serpell, J., In the company of animals: A Study of Human-Animal Relationships, Cambridge University Press, 1996

with the outside world an ability has been suggested to have a practical application in therapy.[4]

PETS AS THERAPY (PAT)

I have grown up with some very memorable and special pets, but Mr Mutley has surpassed them all, and now I will tell you how this book came about and what sparked my interest in animal therapy. Some people believe that pets actually choose their owners and, in Mutley's case, he certainly chose to live with me and as a result has become indispensable. He's not just a companion and work mate, he is almost an extension of me and has enriched lives in ways only dog lovers can comprehend.

Mutley was, quite literally, an accident. An unplanned pregnancy almost discovered too late! His mother Tilly lives on the dairy farm round the corner and I often walked her with my loopy Dalmatian Hector. Tilly was becoming podgy which was strange for a dog that never stopped, and as a result was walked more and her meals cut down. It was only when the vet came to check on a calf that he commented 'How long has she got?' and it was discovered she had a tummy full of puppies. She had just two weeks to be fattened back up and prepared for motherhood! Miraculously, they were all born healthy and happy, shiny little black pups – Mutley being the only boy – and at once I knew he was mine. It was an odd feeling as I had seen countless other litters in the village and never even considered having another dog but Mutley was different. It was

4 Corson, 1981, cited in Serpell, J., *In the Company of Animals: A study of Human-Animal Relationships*, Cambridge University Press, 1996

just one of those 'knowing' instances – the type when you are house hunting and 'just know' when you find the perfect home.

The plan was to train him up like his father as a gun dog (unbeknown to anyone, Tilly had jumped out of the windows of the kitchen where she was kept while in season and had nipped over to see Ebony, a beautiful black working Labrador, who lived opposite!). Initially, Mutley was perfect: he had the instinct and was so quick and eager to learn. When he was ten months old, I took him on the last day of the season, really to check that he was not gun-shy and to show him off on the last drive. But gun-shy was not the issue, he was instead 'pheasant' shy – he wouldn't go near the dead birds and as for the flappers, he was terrified! It became a bit of a joke and I promised to toughen him up for the next season. However, he was worse: he refused to pick up the birds; he was perfect with dummies and dummies wrapped in feathers, but when it came to the real thing, he was so uncomfortable. Instead, he dragged them with the very tip of their extended wing in his mouth and licked them, seemingly trying to bring them back to life! Being a gun dog just wasn't for him! Mutley was more intent on cheering up the cold guns and beaters. He has the most expressive face – more so than any other dog I have had – he knows exactly what you are saying, or feeling, and cuddles up beside you in the perfect way only animals can do. In fact, Mutley was such a great dog that I wanted to share him, so after an interview and temperament test he was accepted as a Pets as Therapy (PAT) dog. So, just as I'd promised them at the farm, he was still going to be a working dog, only a different sort.

PAT is a national charity which has a number of volunteers

who provide therapeutic visits to hospitals, hospices, nursing and care homes, special needs schools and a variety of other venues by sharing their own friendly, temperament-tested and vaccinated pet dogs and cats. The charity was established in 1983 and there are currently 3,500 visiting dogs and ninety visiting cats in the UK. Since its beginning, over 18,000 dogs have been registered into the PAT scheme. Every week, these calm friendly dogs and cats give more than 10,000 people, young and old, the pleasure and chance to cuddle and talk to them. The bedsides visited each year number a staggering half a million.

Visits can be summed up in this comment written by PAT volunteer, Bronwyn Pendray:

> 'When we take [the dogs] on PAT visits, the residents' eyes light up, even those who most of the time are not with it. They tell my husband and me stories of when they owned a dog, and how much they loved them. Many who are too old to move will stroke our dogs when we hold them up to them. I am also assistant junior leader for PAT Dogs. Our juniors have many problems, some are dog phobic and some very shy, but the dogs being very gentle have helped them all. One little girl was so frightened of dogs she couldn't even look at them, but now she accompanies me to the residential home and has control of one of the dogs. It does your heart good to see what benefit owning an animal can have…'

Little research has been carried out to look specifically at the benefits of such visits but this must not mar us into thinking that it lessens the significance and importance of such visits. The majority of existing research into the psychological benefits of animals simply looks at the effects of *owning* a pet rather than having one visit as a one-off or regular occurrence.

As part of their work, Pets As Therapy wanted to look into the effects of their animals visiting on the mood state of participants from nursing homes and day-care centres – that is, people who do not have their own pets – to see if a visiting animal had similar effects and altered their mood state. As defined by the *Oxford English Dictionary*, mood state can be 'the existing condition of a state of mind or feeling' – meaning it can therefore be positive or negative. Mood states may also include a number of different aspects such as fatigue, depression, anxiety and hostility, and thus can be described as one aspect of psychological wellbeing.

The experiment used typical short-term therapy whereby a volunteer and their own dog visited people for a short period of time of around ten minutes per person. It explored the differences in mood state of people in a nursing home or day-care centre before and after PAT visits. These differences were measured using the profile of mood states questionnaire (McNaire et al, 1981) with six levels: depression, anxiety, tiredness, feeling unsure, confusion and hostility. Control groups were also used in the nursing home and day-care centre conditions, which looked at whether any differences in mood state occurred without Pets As Therapy dogs present. The hospital anxiety and depression scale (Zigmond and Snaith, 1983) was used to compare participants' initial levels of anxiety and depression, and screened participants to ensure there were no extreme differences in anxiety and depression.

A total of fifty-two participants were used in the study. Twenty-seven of them received Pets As Therapy visits in the nursing homes and day-care centres; fifteen were male and twelve female. The age range in this condition was 62–89 and the mean age was 79. Institutions were initially contacted to ask their permission for research to take place there. At the individual institutions, participants were a convenience sample recruited personally by the experimenter. It was also necessary to check that none of the recruited participants suffered from dementia.

There were twenty-five participants in the nursing home and day-centre control condition (no Pets As Therapy visits). Of these, fourteen were female and eleven were male. The age range was 71–95 with a mean age of 84. These participants were allocated to this control group randomly. All of the participants were British and English was their first language. Participants were also screened using the Hospital Anxiety and Depression scale (Zigmond and Snaith, 1983). This ensured that none of the participants experienced very high levels of anxiety or depression.

So, summing up the study,[5] just over half of the participants received a visit from Pets As Therapy, while the other half took part in the control conditions and did not receive a Pets As Therapy visit.

The results were conclusive and showed that there was a significant positive effect from the Pets As Therapy visits on the profile of mood states scores in both the nursing home and day-

5 The effects of brief Pets As Therapy visits on mood state in nursing homes and day centres – conducted by Claire Taylor, with PAT volunteers Jane Ambler (PAT dogs Bonaparte, Cognac and Jamey) and Catherine Corey (PAT dog Boone)

care setting. This linked with other research mentioned in the introduction to this book about the positive effect of owning a pet thus shows the presence of animals improves the mood state of humans regardless of the participants' environment.

PAT runs an annual Dog of the Year competition which, along with the incredible acts all PAT animals do on a day-to-day basis, highlights extra-special PAT stories. For example, Cassie, who is owned by Ruth Boyes from Dewsbury, regularly visits the Manor Croft Nursing Home and Dewsbury District Hospital. Residents at the nursing home explained: 'Tuesday is the best day of the week because that's when Cassie comes to visit and she helps us feel better'. Staff said, 'Cassie is such a good therapist for us all,' and wrote the following poem:

> Vote for Cassie as PAT Dog of the Year
> To so many she brings warmth and cheer
> With her grizzly coat and floppy ear
> She is a friend who many hold dear.
> Even when you are sad and low
> She'll lift your spirit and make your heart glow.
> If you need a silent friend, she always knows
> With each passing visit, the friendship grows
> Eyebrows which dance up and down
> Expressions that take away your frown.
> When Cassie's around, you cannot be sad
> When she comes to visit us, we all feel glad.

Not all PAT dogs are small lap dogs either, as Becky shows. Owned by Margaret Thomson from Dundee, she is a large Rottweiler and visits at both Camperdown Care Home and

Ballumbie Nursing Home, who say, 'As a fully grown Rottweiller, Becky is perhaps not everyone's idea of a PAT Dog, but spend five minutes with her and anyone can see that she is the ideal choice. Becky works in a home for clients with learning difficulties and has to deal with a lot of distractions including very high levels of noise. Every week for the past eight years, Becky has brought smiles to the faces of all our residents and even helped one overcome his great fear of dogs. To many of our residents, Becky is the closest any of them will come to having a pet and she has become a valuable and much-loved member of Camperdown's family. This is an invaluable service.'

Similarly, Manny is a very special Great Dane owned by Patricia Hanratty from Wakefield, in West Yorkshire. Manny visits Ward P at Pinderfields Hospital, where Jackie Wright is a staff nurse and nominated Manny as PAT Dog of the Year saying,

> 'We love it when Dr Manny visits as he really cheers up the patients. We recently had a gentleman on the ward who had been unwell for a week, not speaking with anyone, barely eating and drinking, but after a twenty-minute visit from Dr Manny the patient became more interested in his surroundings and began to eat and drink again – his family were amazed. This is only one of many examples and shows how positive Pets As Therapy is for patients. Manny has a special place in our hearts.'

Manny's story is even more special when you consider that when he was just six months old he was diagnosed with a rare heart complaint. Ultimately he had to have heart surgery. He thoroughly enjoys his visit to the hospital and when the patients compare operation scars, Manny always wins paws down!

Taz is a West Highland White Terrier who is owned by Freda Arblaster from Walsall, in Staffordshire, and visits several residential homes. Activities organisers Jenny and Sarah at Lakeside said, 'From the day we met Taz it was like a breath of fresh air had stepped into Lakeside Residential Home. Taz is a wonderful little dog who is hard-working, well-behaved and sometimes comical. If you could see how much he lights up our residents' faces, you would be lost for words. Taz is a dog in a million and has become part of Lakesides' family.' Chris Carr, from The Lake's Nursing Home calls Taz 'a real little treasure'.

Kola, owned by Cynthia Pitts from Crawley, in Sussex, was nominated by staff and children at Manor Green College, where the students have special needs. Some pupils have a range of learning disabilities and some also have physical disabilities. Staff from the college say, 'He is a delightful PAT dog and welcome any time'.

Moss, a Border Collie owned by Trish Weatherley from Hextable, in Kent, visits Willow Ward, a children's ward at Darent Valley Hospital in Kent, and the nomination came from the staff on the ward: 'Moss has a tremendous effect on the children's wellbeing. He brings smiles to the faces of children and adults alike.' The nomination reads: 'He is fun, entertaining, gentle and patient, and seems to sense that the children are not feeling well. Everyone looks forward to Moss's visits and we are extremely grateful to Trish, his owner, for bringing Moss to our ward.'

CHILDREN IN HOSPITAL AND ANIMAL THERAPY ASSOCIATION (CHATA)

Similarly, there is the organisation called Children in Hospital and Animal Therapy Association which was founded by Sandra and Ronnie Stone in 1995 and is simply devoted to 'putting a smile on the face of very sick children'. Sandra, a children's nurse for twenty-one years, was helping a friend take two dog 'visitors' round an elderly people's home when she was struck by the impact the animals had on everyone. 'As we made our way around the room, the level of conversation rose and there was a wonderful atmosphere – everyone just looked so much happier,' she says. 'We were about to leave when I noticed a gentleman sitting a little away from everyone else. He had only said half a dozen words in all the months he had been there.'

When Sandra took the dogs up to him 'it was like opening the floodgates. He started to feel them, running his hands down their bodies, putting his arms around their necks, talking to them. He began to talk about dogs he had owned. It was very, very moving and it really made me think about the value of animals. Those dogs were the key to releasing so many emotions,' she says. Like all mothers, Sandra had often used the family pets to treat tears. As she watched the old man emerge from his solitary world, she became convinced that animals could be used to help seriously ill children. 'I realised there was so much untapped opportunity for therapy,' she explains. She approached a number of London hospitals. Some welcomed the diversion but wanted to keep the animals in a playroom. 'If you put animals in that setting, they're seen as toys; children want to dress them up or put bandages on them. That's not what we're about,' says Sandra firmly.

Dr Melinda Edwards, a consultant paediatric psychologist who has pioneered animal therapy in the children's wards of Guy's Hospital, London, agrees. 'They're much more than a play item or a distraction,' she says. 'I witness so many benefits. When children are in hospital for a long time they lose contact with what it is like to be an ordinary child – everything focuses on their body and treatment. Animals allow them to be ordinary for a while.'

Every week CHATA volunteers take animals to Guy's and visits are arranged to make sure they are targeted at the children most in need – some long-term patients, many terminally ill. Animals have helped to rouse youngsters from comas and are even taken into the intensive care unit. On one occasion, a little girl who needed a heart transplant agreed to surgery only on the condition that she could see a chinchilla when she came round – CHATA fixed it and she has now fully recovered.

Kirsty Reid doesn't have a lot to smile about. The bone in her right thigh snapped when she and her disabled mother were hit by a car on a pedestrian crossing. She will need six or seven weeks in traction and many more weeks of physiotherapy before she can walk properly again. Today though, the eleven-year-old is beaming as a special visitor pads into the Kingfisher Unit at Chase Farm Hospital in north London. 'Shh, don't tell the nurses,' she whispers conspiratorially as a blanket is laid out on her bed and Shadow, an immaculately groomed Border Collie, leaps up beside her. Actually, the nurses are in on the secret! Shadow, Willow the rabbit, and guinea pigs Laa Laa and Po are regular visitors to the Kingfisher Unit. The animals are brought in by volunteers from CHATA and they are as much a part of ward routine as doctors' rounds and meal trolleys.

Shadow is quite simply a 'miracle worker' according to Hilda Reid, Kirsty's mother. 'The first time the dog had been there I couldn't believe the change. Kirsty had been miserable for a week and in an awful lot of pain. After she'd seen Shadow, there was a complete transformation, as if someone had taken away the sad Kirsty and brought back a completely different child.'

At first there had been doubts about the animals transmitting infection, but they are thoroughly checked by vets and Sandra follows a strict protocol agreed with each hospital's infection control unit. If ward visits cannot be arranged, children who are well enough to leave hospital can also take part in day trips and outings organised around animals.

A study is now being set up at Guy's to try and pinpoint just how animals can exert such a positive influence on our health. Melinda Edwards believes the volunteers (all of whom must have childcare, teaching or medical experience) also play an important role. 'It's not enough to have the animal and child, you need a skilled adult facilitator to pick up on things the child says and relate that back to them.' For instance, a child who comforts an animal may be acting out their own anxiety. By gently drawing them out – asking what frightens the animal, for instance – volunteers can encourage children to voice their own fears. Often it is a case of recognising an oblique reference to an incident that has upset the youngster – a clumsily taken blood test, for instance, or a harassed medic not finding time to explain things fully. Sandra believes the animals help give control back to the child. 'When an animal comes onto the ward the child's role changes – they become the carer, not the patient being cared for. The child can feed and groom it, even if it's only for fifteen minutes. It is also a focus for the child to talk about their own pets, or experiences with animals. They can direct the conversation, not simply answer questions about their illness or injury.' Dr Edwards says, 'For some children, life is a horror movie which they can't switch off and they just get totally unresponsive, but Sandra putting rabbits on the bed and chatting away can turn a totally unresponsive child into a positive outgoing one. Animals break down barriers.'

In some cases, animals can get through when nothing else can. The children of a Vietnamese refugee family were eight, six and four when Sandra first met them. They had witnessed terrible hardship during their escape and then suffered at the hands of a violent father. At a safe haven, all three elected to become mute. They would not communicate with their mother, their teachers, other children or even with each other. A CHATA rabbit made them smile for the first time but it was the squeaky noises of a guinea pig that really hit the mark! 'I started telling them what each noise meant – I made it up half the time – and the children began to imitate them,' remembers Sandra. 'They began to speak in whispers at first to each other and then to their mother.' They are now all back at school, joining in happily[6].

ANIMALS AROUND THEIR SICK OWNERS

The fact that animals feel our pain, our joy and our stress should come as no surprise to anyone who has a pet. Whether

6 http://www.ezio.freeserve.co.uk/magic.htm

we recognise it or not, the emotional as well as the physical environment we create has a direct impact on the way our pets behave. Dr Schoen states that, 'we emit energetic signals related to our deepest feelings that are picked up by those around us – especially our pets.' The emotional benefits from animals are difficult to measure, meaning that pets help humans without anyone knowing exactly why. What experts know, however, is that animals allow humans to focus, even for a short period of time, on something other than themselves.

Reading Sharon Osbourne's biography *Extreme*, one can see the huge part dogs play in her life, but more interestingly, it was when she underwent treatment for colon cancer that the special bond between Sharon and Minnie the Pomeranian intensified, as Minnie refused to leave her side the entire time, curling up next to her in bed, day in, day out. Doctors were concerned about the risk of infection but, as Sharon said, she would not have got through it without Minnie.

Such stories of pets caring for their owners are certainly not unique – Bronwyn Pendray wrote to me about the period when she was recovering from breast cancer: 'My dogs sensed I was ill, they followed me everywhere and sat by my side when I was crying. I cuddled them to feel safe (silly, I know) – they helped me through the biggest fight of my life.'

Similarly, we know some pets will treat their pregnant owner with more attention and care than usual. One woman had a difficult pregnancy and ended up on bed rest. Her dog refused to leave her side and had to be forcefully pushed outside to go and spend a penny!

Nicola Smith's German shorthaired Pointer-Labrador cross

Holly has provided incredible support to Nicola who has agoraphobia. For nearly a year, she was too scared to go outside and was practically a prisoner in her own home. Holly sits with Nicola when she feels nervous or has a panic attack and brings her her mobile phone if needed. She has become Nicola's best friend and constant companion, and has stopped her being afraid of everyday things like being outside, in crowds or alone. As a result, Nicola has grown in confidence and independence[7].

Also, rescue dog Shadow is a great companion to owner Jessica Muckelt of Broughton Astley, Leicester, who has Aspergers Syndrome – a form of autism – and has improved her confidence in communicating with other humans[8].

All round, pets are good for our emotional and physical health. Caring for a companion animal can provide a sense of purpose and fulfilment and lessen feelings of loneliness and isolation in all age groups. It is well known that relaxed, happy people do not become ill as often as those who suffer from stress and depression.

Animal companionship also helps lower a person's blood pressure and cholesterol levels. And studies show that having a dog increases survival rates in groups of patients who have suffered cardiac arrest. Dog walking, pet grooming and even petting all provide increased physical activity that strengthens the heart, improves blood circulation and slows the loss of bone tissue. Put simply, pets are not just good friends, they are good medicine.

7 Friends for Life Competition – Crufts 2006
8 *ibid*

DOLPHIN-ASSISTED THERAPY

Animals also provide healing outside pet-assisted therapies in hospital and domestic settings: with dolphin therapy, horseback riding, farm-animal and wildlife interaction and marine life activity, to name but some.

Dolphin Assisted Therapy (DAT) is a new and exciting field of modern medicine that some people categorise as part of animal therapy. This field of medicine has shown extraordinary results and breakthroughs in outcomes in relation to the conventional methods of treatments, such as prescribed medication, human therapy, and so on. It is relatively new, but already has documented results in patients who choose to try it.

Dolphin therapy is already used to help children undergoing rehabilitation for a range of conditions as well as for the sick and disabled. The technique had also been shown to aid young people with Attention Deficit Hyperactivity Disorder (ADHD) and older people with dementia.

Swimming with dolphins has even been reported to help alleviate mild to moderate depression. A University of Leicester team tested the effect of regular swimming sessions with dolphins on fifteen depressed people in a study carried out in Honduras over a two-week period. The study, published in the *British Medical Journal*, stated that symptoms improved more among the group who swam and snorkelled around dolphins for one hour a day than among another fifteen who swam in the same area but did not interact with dolphins. All the volunteers who took part in the trial stopped taking antidepressant drugs or undergoing psychotherapy at least four weeks beforehand.

The researchers say the dolphins' aesthetic value and the emotions raised by the interaction may have healing properties. Some have speculated that the ultrasound emitted by dolphins as part of their echo location system may have a beneficial effect. The Leicester team believe that using animals in this way could be a productive way to treat depression and other psychiatric illnesses. Researcher Professor Michael Reveley said, 'Dolphins are highly intelligent animals who are capable of complex interactions, and regard humans positively. Some people who are depressed may have issues with other humans, and might respond more positively to other types of interaction. We need to remember that we are part of the natural world, and interacting with it can have a beneficial effect on us[9].'

It was concluded that 'swimming with and caring for dolphins as a group activity in a vacation context is very likely therefore to alleviate depression'. However, it was said that researchers would probably do better to focus their efforts on animal interactions that were more readily available closer to home.

BIRTHING AND DOLPHINS

Dolphins are well known to be curious about pregnant women and often come around to check them out. This is a common occurrence according to Dean Bernal, companion to the free dolphin JoJo, who swims with many people in the Turks and Caicos Islands. For this reason, in commercial 'swim with dolphin' programmes, pregnant ladies are often excluded from

9 25 November 2005, BBC News http://news.bbc.co.uk/2/hi/health/4465998.stm

the swims because the dolphins often concentrate their attention on them to the exclusion of the other paying clients!

Underwater birth is an accepted part of the British health services and recommended for those who anticipate problems with their pregnancy and hundreds of thousands of successful underwater births have occurred throughout the world. The initial enthusiasm for this technique has grown and its benefits for the mother and child are increasingly confirmed. Now here comes the twist... Running parallel to these developments is the practice of dolphin-assisted therapy, which was developed through the work of Dr Hank Truby, Dr Betsy Smith, Dr David Nathanson, David Cole, Scott Taylor, Dr Horace Dobbs, MD, et alia. The direct experience of many people who have encountered dolphins is that they have in some way been healed, or had their conditions improved[10].

As the advantages of underwater birth became clear, and the therapeutic value of dolphins was demonstrated, the concept of humans giving birth underwater with dolphins developed. Since birthing in water is beneficial and dolphins are able to heal or improve a wide range of medical conditions, it is reasonable to suppose that their presence at water births could be beneficial.

Some twenty years ago, after developing and confirming the benefits of water birth, Igor Tscharkofsy began to deliver human babies in the Black Sea with dolphins. Some of the reported occurrences include a mother and a baby playing with the dolphins within forty-five minutes of the birth and there is another instance of a free dolphin escorting a newborn human baby to the surface for its first breath. According to Igor

10 See: http:///www.planetpuna.com/dp.htm

Smirnoff, their research director, water babies develop six months faster over their first two years and the development of walking and talking occurs earlier. Elena Tonetti, who managed the Black Sea birth project for several years, reports that the water babies are also more likely to become ambidextrous, too.

DOGS AND CANCER

In September 2004, the *British Medical Journal* (BMJ) published the results of ground-breaking research which proved the theory that cancer produces chemicals with distinctive odours which dogs, using their exceptional sense of smell, can detect. Since its publication, the research and project have received worldwide acclaim.

Animals are also helping humans in the fight against cancer. Anecdotal evidence is plentiful about dogs alerting their owners to cancerous lumps and growths. Gill Lacey who is very much involved with the Hearing Dogs for Deaf People charity can provide one such account. Her Dalmatian Trudii alerted her to a malignant melanoma back in 1978, effectively saving her life. Trudii became obsessed with a small mole on her leg, getting to the point where she was actually trying to nip it off! It was then that Gill decided she needed to get over her inhibitions and consult her GP. Although the mole looked totally normal, the doctor decided to remove it under local anaesthetic and send it off for tests. The results came back saying that it was in fact a malignant melanoma, a very aggressive form of skin cancer, so Gill had to have a much larger area of surrounding tissue removed to take it away. Over thirty years later, she is still alive and well, and now edits *Favour*, the magazine for the charity.

In 1989 and 2001 letters were published in the *Lancet* medical journal outlining similar cases to Gill's. The, in 2002, Dr John Church, a retired orthopaedic surgeon and co-author of one of the letters, made a television appeal for help in training dogs for a scientific study. Gill suggested some of the Hearing Dogs team could help with this in their spare time as they had experience in training the hearing dogs as well as gundogs, and at this point Andy Cook and Claire Guest got involved as dog trainers.

Dr Church's dream was to establish a team and to statistically create a proper study to show a dog's ability to detect cancer by its smell. Next, he persuaded the Dermatology department at Amersham Hospital to take part, which was represented by research scientist Dr Carolyn Willis.

The original plan was to test the ability of dogs to detect skin cancer. However, as urine samples could be made available more readily than tissue samples, they decided instead to measure the dog's ability to detect bladder cancer. Once their proposal and strict protocol was passed by the hospital's ethics committee, Claire and Andy, along with two colleagues – Sandra Stevenson and Jan Smith – began to train six dogs, none of whom had any prior experience in scent discrimination, over seven months to distinguish between urine samples from bladder cancer patients and those from healthy people and individuals with non-cancerous diseases for the study. These dogs were their own pets, not selected or carefully bred for the task, and they were doing the research in their own time. Meetings often went on into the late hours as they agonised over the progress of their dogs. As trainers, they decided to key the dogs into the scent of urine samples from a variety of patients with bladder cancer in the hope that they would identify the 'cancer ingredient'. The dogs were taught to ignore the scents of other urological diseases. In this way, they could prove that the dogs were detecting cancer specifically and not just disease in general.

The dogs seemed to be doing brilliantly, but just as they were entering the final stages of training, they suffered a huge setback. One by one, the dogs identified a supposedly cancer-free sample as if it were positive. Having tried but failed to convince the dogs to ignore this sample, they became extremely despondent. The hospital decided to call back the relevant patient for further tests and discovered a bladder-type cancer in one of the patient's kidneys, following which it was successfully treated. The dogs had been right after all – it was the boost they needed and still with more training to do, they had already saved someone's life!

For research to be credible, it needs to take place under very strict conditions in a controlled setting. On the morning of the first day of tests, the hospital delivered a whole new set of urine samples from patients the dogs had not encountered before, including non-cancer patients with many diseases of which the dogs had no experience. Each dog was offered a set of seven urine samples and their task was to determine which of them was from a patient with bladder cancer. All the samples were encoded so no one knew which was which.

As Andy said, 'It was nerve-wracking. Each dog worked nine lines, indicating a positive sample by lying down next to it.

During the fortnight of testing we had no idea whether the dogs were making the correct decisions or not,'[11] It took several more days for the code to be cracked and the results to be compiled.

The dogs, comprising three Spaniels, one Papillon, one Labrador and one mongrel, correctly selected the bladder cancer urine on twenty-two out of fifty-four occasions – an average success rate of 41 per cent (the best dogs achieving 56 per cent) compared to the 14 per cent which would have been expected if the dogs had randomly selected a sample each time. This was statistically significant and the statistician and the hospital were delighted. The trainers were initially disappointed, though, that the dogs' performances had dropped during the controlled test from the 95 per cent success rate that they were achieving in training. But, as each dog was encountering sixty-three new test samples, some with diseases they had not been trained to exclude, it was to be expected.

Dr John Church was not surprised at the results of the study. 'I am a passionate believer that animals have a huge amount to teach us, and I have heard many stories of people who have been alerted to the presence of cancer in their bodies by their pet dogs. I was delighted to find that the two charities were open minded enough to participate in this study, so that we could really examine this phenomenon scientifically.'

Having the study accepted for publication in the *BMJ* gave the whole project authenticity and worldwide acclaim, but there is still a long way to go. 'We were flattered to be asked to

11 Material adapted with permission from Gill Lacey and Andy Cook, original information and statistics taken from Hearing Dogs press releases and an article 'Cancer Detection Dogs' published by Hearing Dogs in Spring/Summer 2005 edition of *Favour* magazine

assist in this study on the basis of our reputation in the field of training dogs,' said Claire Guest, operations director at Hearing Dogs, 'Although we have been very careful not to let this project affect our normal work, which involves training dogs for deaf people. The four of us who trained these cancer detection dogs did so using our own pet dogs, in our own homes, in our own spare time.'

Inspired by their success in this first pilot study, the group are already making plans for conducting further research, with the aim of pushing back the boundaries of knowledge in this crucial area. To this end, two new young dogs – Flo and Oak – have already commenced training alongside their older, four-footed friends.

CHAPTER 8

Life-Saving Pets

When man is in trouble, God sends him a dog.
ALPHONSE DE LARMARTINE

Here, we look at pets and animals who have gone beyond the call of duty or their training and saved the lives of their owners. There are countless tales around, including dogs who dive underwater to pull their trapped owner out from under a canoe, or dogs who jump off cliffs to save their owners, or pets waking owners to warn them of fires and natural disasters.

Then there are cases of dogs who are credited by police, such as Dante, who befriended a man who allegedly set out to embark on a widespread killing spree. The friendly, four-and-a-half-year-old, neutered male Husky-Australian Shepherd cross was honoured as the first-ever recipient of the coveted Animal Heroes Award at a special ceremony by the Humane Society of Canada. It was late June, and a troubled forty-four-year-old man, later identified as James Paul Stanson, was driving around the Beaches area in the east of Toronto with an arsenal of weapons in his vehicle, including a rifle with a telescopic scope, a 12-gauge shotgun, a 9-mm semi-automatic handgun, a machete, a throwing knife, camouflage ski mask, black leather gloves and over 6,296 rounds of ammunition.

Stanson's alleged plan for mass murder was derailed by an encounter with the friendly, lovable dog named Dante who was out for an afternoon stroll with his owner, Kristina Kyser, and her six-week-old baby: 'Dante ran up to a large man wearing a windbreaker, who began petting him. I could tell right away that the man obviously liked dogs. I went into shock when I saw his sketch in the papers afterwards and realised who the man was.'

When he turned himself in to police later that afternoon, Stanson told the officers that his encounter with this friendly dog made him have second thoughts about his alleged plan. 'It basically could have gone either way,' said Detective Nick Ashley.

DOGS ON THE TITANIC

RMS *Titanic* was the largest liner in the world. She arrived in Southampton from her builders, Harland and Wolff, in Belfast, on the morning of 4 April 1912. There, she prepared for her maiden voyage and was due to sail on the 10th of that month. The *Titanic* was the flagship of the White Star Line, founded by Thomas Ismay in 1869, the shipping line had been quick to establish a reputation for speed, comfort, safety and size.

Titanic was known as the 'ship of dreams'. The luxury and workmanship that had gone into this great ship was far superior to anything tried before and the crowning feature of the *Titanic*'s interior was the grand staircase that had a great wrought-iron-and-glass dome overhead. Victorian society flocked to be part of the epic maiden voyage, but fate was to play a cruel hand a few days after the ship left Southampton's waters.

The story is well known. Indeed, the world has become fascinated with the tragedy. Speeding through the night in an attempt to reach New York in record time, the *Titanic* hit an iceberg that resulted in an horrific loss of life and the destruction of the ship that was supposed to be unsinkable. The human tragedy and bravery of that night are well-documented. Perhaps not so well-documented, though, are the stories of the dogs that were on board when *Titanic* sank. Some of the accounts are confused but the following information appears in a variety of respected accounts of that fateful night.

It was not unusual for small dogs, 'lap dogs', to accompany their owners on a sea cruise. Indeed, a dog show had been planned on board *Titanic*, for Monday 15 April. The dogs ranged from a Chow owned by Harry Anderson, to a champion French Bulldog owned by Robert Daniels and valued at £750. The Astors, the *Titanic*'s most prominent passengers, had their Airedale named Kitty with them.

Although the kennel facilities on *Titanic* were excellent, Frou-Frou, a tiny pet belonging to Helen Bishop, stayed and slept in her owner's cabin. Each day, a member of *Titanic*'s crew would take the huge variety of dogs for a walk. The parade was quite a spectacle.

Of all the dogs on the *Titanic*, it is suggested that only two survived. One was a Pomeranian owned by Miss Margaret Hays of New York, who tucked the dog inside her coat and got into lifeboat number seven. The other was a Pekinese named Sun Yat Sen, and owned by Henry Sleeper, who boarded lifeboat number three with his master. Because both lifeboats were nearly empty as they were released from *Titanic*, no one objected to the dogs being there.

It is documented that a passenger went below and released all the dogs from the kennels before *Titanic* disappeared beneath the waves. Some accounts speak of a Newfoundland, who saved a woman's life by dragging her to a lifeboat before expiring itself. There are tales of Rigel, another Newfoundland belonging to the *Titanic*'s first officer, swimming in the freezing sea in a desperate attempt to find his master. Rigel's story goes on to say that he prevented the *Carpathia* from missing a lifeboat with survivors too weak to identify their location by barking until someone heard him and the people were saved. This suggests three dogs were saved, as Rigel apparently was taken on board the *Carpathia* and given medical attention and food. It should be remembered that the water temperature at that time was such that any human's or dog's survival was a miracle.

The 'ship of dreams' was found in 1985 by an underwater expedition. *Titanic*'s story still fascinates millions of people around the world. The loss of human life was colossal and those people should never be forgotten. Perhaps sometimes the loss of those other, well-loved little creatures should also be given a moment's thought because they are part of *Titanic*'s story, too.[1]

---

1 http://homepage.ntlworld.com/k.westgate/history3.htm

ALERTING HUMANS TO DANGER

THE FIRE ALARM GOAT

Katie used to work as a herdswoman on a dairy and she also had a pet goat, who lived in the same building as the calves, which was directly next to the farmhouse and part of the barn. One winter, they had been disbudding the calves (so they don't grow horns) with an electric disbudding iron, and had finished and left everything safe, bearing in mind that the barn was full of straw. Katie had moved onto doing something totally different and can distinctly remember the dreadful noise that Muffy her pet goat was making. The sound was out of this world – really weird, and made her think that she was being strangled! Straightaway, Katie ran over to the calf house and realised that the iron had just started to create a flame. It was unplugged and, as she said, 'We're not daft, we had placed it well out the way to cool down, so to this day we don't know what happened. But the goat sensed it and alerted us to it – left alone it would have started a fire and then who knows what would have happened?'

STARKEY AND THE COOKER

And it's not just goats with a sixth sense and the intelligence to warn us of fires. Pauline Byrne from Kent wrote to me about one of her cats:

'Many years ago, when my boys and I lived in London we had a cat called Starkey. One day, when I was upstairs, I had put something on the cooker and my younger son was in the front room, when Starkey kept biting his hand while he was drawing on the floor. Eventually, Mark followed him into the kitchen to find the cooker alight. I was able to get down the stairs and put the fire out, but had it not been for Starkey attracting Mark's attention, it could have been a lot worse.'

FRASER AND THE CHILDREN

Yorkshire terrier cross Fraser is one of the smallest working Hearing Dogs and although he has only been with Dawn a short time, he has already helped the whole family. Dawn explains what Fraser did:

'I have not had Fraser that long and he is still in training but he has changed my life so much. I am profoundly deaf and have three small children. Two of those children have special needs, the youngest one is also deaf.

'Fraser came into our lives just after Christmas last year. One morning I was upstairs in a bedroom. My daughter Emily, who is four, was upstairs and went to the toilet. I did not hear her. The next thing I knew was that Fraser was tapping at my leg as if he was trying to tell me something – a bit like he does when the doorbell goes. This time, though, he was tapping me very hard and in a different way as if it was urgent, as if he knew something was wrong. I asked him, "What is it?" He showed me and I followed him, he took me to the hall of the upstairs landing to Emily. It was then that I saw Emily had collapsed at the top of the stairs crying in pain.

'We took her to the hospital and she is still having tests. The doctors asked her what had happened and she said that she had a very bad pain in her tummy. She had cried very softly and Fraser had come to her. She can remember *him licking her face and then she knew he would go and get me. So she knew she was safe. The doctors and nurses were amazed when she told them that.*

'I am so proud of Fraser for doing that because I have always worried about not hearing the children. My other daughter – who is three – has only one kidney, which is not working well. She is often very ill and cries. It used to worry me that one day or night I would not hear her when she needed me, but I don't need to worry now as I have my heroic dog Fraser.'

CRIME BUSTING PIG!

In 1993, in Houston, Texas, Mona, a 200-lb (91-kg) pig, became a crime-buster. A burglar running away from police had leapt into Mona's pen. She grabbed the crook by the leg and held him until police officers arrived![2]

CAT THWARTS A CAT BURGLAR

Sandi Arnold was up late one night. It was the early hours and with a hard frost predicted, she decided to cover her geraniums. When she came in, she didn't lock the door. A few minutes later, she thought perhaps she heard something outside, but did not think much of it. Frankie Joe, her cat, came running over and looked up at her.

'He was running in place as he nervously looked back and forth between me and the back storm door. 'What is it, Frankie Joe? What's wrong?' I asked him. Sandi ran to look out the back door and found a man with a stocking cap pulled down low was at the back door. Once he saw her, he took off,

2 http://lava.nationalgeographic.com/cgi-bin/aow/aow.cgi?day=26&month=1&year=02

running. As she said, 'There is no doubt in my mind that given a minute more, that man would have entered my home. Frankie Joe saved my life.'[3]

Yorkshire terrier Poppy Lou[4] tugged at Victoria Shaw's nightie until she woke up at her Rhos-y-medre bungalow near Wrexham, Wales, in November. The council house gas fire was leaking deadly carbon monoxide and would have killed her had it not been for her pet. The gas fire had been on all that day on Thursday 24 November 2005 and Victoria had begun to feel tired, her eyes started to itch and so she went to bed. Luckily for Victoria, though, Poppy Lou cried, licked and scratched her face, and tugged her nightie until she woke up, alerting her to the poisonous fumes. As Victoria said, 'If it wasn't for Poppy Lou, I wouldn't be here. She is all I have and it is fantastic.'[5]

PROTECTING AND SAVING HUMAN LIVES

RAPID RESCUE

In 1982, Rob and Laurie Roberts set out in their dory (a small, shallow boat) down the Colorado River, near their home. They took along Bo, their Labrador-Retriever. In the rapids, a wave flipped the dory. Rob made it to shore, but Laurie was trapped under the boat. Twice Bo dived for her. The second time, he pulled Laurie up by her hair. She grabbed Bo's tail and

3 Adapted from http://www.rd.com/content/openContent.do?contentId=18647

4 Poppy Lou was nominated for the Kennel Club's Friends for Life parade which was held on 12 March 2006 at the NEC in Birmingham

5 www.icnorthwales.co.uk Life-saving pet honoured with place in dog parade. posted 14 February 2006

he towed her to shore. Bo was named Ken-L Ration Dog Hero in 1982.[6]

THE FARMERS' PROTECTIVE HERD

Cows often appear to be very slow creatures but in 1996 a herd in Carmarthen, in west Wales, acted fast to save a farmer. A bull weighing 1.5 tons attacked farmer Donald Mottram, hurling him to the ground and stomping on him. Donald lay unconscious for ninety minutes. When he awoke, the astonished farmer saw his cows surrounding him – protecting him from the aggressive, snorting bull. Led by his favourite cow, Daisy, the herd continued guarding him as he crawled to the fence and safety.[7]

JOSH AND THE COWS

Mr and Mrs Dudley from Welford on Avon were walking their dog Josh along the river when they saw a herd of about forty young cattle at the other end of the field in which they were walking. Mr Dudley wrote,

> 'Now I know cattle are not normally aggressive but they are quite inquisitive and often they dislike dogs. Suddenly – like a cowboy movie – a charge towards us started. They thundered down towards us and there was nowhere to go except into the river. Josh had had no training for this sort of thing but all I could do was let him off the leash.
> 'He sat for a moment, picked out the leader, ran like

6 http://lava.nationalgeographic.com/cgi-bin/aow/aow.cgi?day=23&month=4&year=0
7 Text by Laura Daily http://lava.nationalgeographic.com/cgi-bin/aow/aow.cgi?day=25&month=1&year=02

the wind and bit it on the front of the leg. The bullock stopped and so did the rest. Josh ran round and round and marshalled them back to where they had been grazing, left them and trotted back to me. I put on his lead and we continued our walk!

'Now I suppose one might say that while he was not trained, these actions are what Collies were bred for, or today we might say they are "in his genes".'

SPARKY AND THE COWS

Similarly, Corrine Douglas was on holiday in Wales and out walking with her dog Sparky, an Ibizan Hound. Sparky had a will of his own and was quite a difficult dog, whom Corrine was finding it hard to bond with, let alone train, and as a result always walked him on a lead. She had walked through a couple of fields and, with Sparky tight on his lead, realised that the next one had a few cows in it. She decided to press on. Besides, Sparky would not affect them close to her on his lead and she was sure the cows would be used to people being with them being on a public footpath, so she climbed over the stile and continued the walk.

The field was large and as she walked along the path, Corrine could see there were more cows on the far side, some with calves. Sparky was behaving and ignoring the cows, more interested in the rabbit smells in the hedge. It was then that one particular cow began walking over towards her – the cow, it turned out, was a young black bullock. This didn't worry Corrine to begin with, she just thought 'Oh, go away you silly thing' and carried on walking, but the bull kept coming and then she realised it was time to run.

The other cows in the field took the bullock's lead and

thundered towards a terrified Corrine. As they crowded around her, she realised there was no escape route back to the stile. It was then that Sparky decided to act. Although on his lead, he stood in front of his mistress attempting to get in between her and the threatening herd, but his gesture was in vain. One of the larger cows hit Corrine square in the ribs, while another was moving to strike at her head. As she lifted her arms to protect herself, she felt the lead slip away. Corrine watched helpless between the cows' legs as Sparky ran off. But instead of running off into the distance, he stopped behind the cows and began to bark, which caught the attention of the cows who were turning towards him.

'I could see him watching me,' she said. He would bark, then run on a bit, then stop and bark. With the cows moving away, Corrine got up and staggered back to the safety of the stile. Suddenly, her thoughts turned to her dog – how would she get him back? He never came when called. But Sparky took the initiative. 'I was a few yards from the stile and he came without me calling him, but to my horror I realised the cows were following him – it seemed his plan had backfired!'

But as the animals bore down on Corrine, Sparky conjured up another remarkable act of intelligence. As soon as they got really close, he ran back out into the field and began barking again. Duly, the cows obliged, turning heel to see what the fuss was about. Corrine made it over the stile and then realised Sparky had jumped over it behind her and both were safe. Hurt, Corrine sat down and found her face was bleeding. She was badly injured and Sparky licked her hands and face showing for the first time ever real affection. As they made their way back to her friend's house, Sparky – who usually pulled on the lead trotted – gently by her side and from that day on, his attitude totally changed. He's become a more relaxed, attentive member of the Douglas family.[8]

DOG AND THE BOAR

A woman attacked by two wild boar was saved by her pet Labrador. Kate Lloyd was walking Harvey in the Forest of Dean in Gloucestershire when she stumbled upon two sows feeding their piglets. On seeing her, the 200-lb beasts charged at her – and Harvey flew into action. Despite being butted five times, Harvey circled Kate until the beasts stomped off. As Kate said, 'When they turned nasty it was terrifying but Harvey was a real hero.'[9]

SCOOTER AND THE RATTLESNAKE

Scooter was a nine-year-old terrier belonging to Patrick Trotter.[10] One afternoon, Patrick was sitting outside on an overturned five-gallon bucket as he worked on a piece of art. He went inside to get a drink and returned to the yard to continue with his work. 'I was just ready to put my foot on the other side of the bucket and didn't even see the four-foot Diamondback snake. Scooter just jumped on my leg and I went flying. The next thing I knew, they were battling it out.'

The snake struck Scooter at jackhammer speed, with over ten puncture wounds found from his mouth down his neck, yet he survived and, in the process, saved his master from being bitten, too. Quite rightly, between 1996 and 1997, Scooter was

---

8 Adapted from Cumming, T. and Wolstencroft, D., *Pet Power*, Ebury Press, 1997, pp. 25–31
9 'A Dog of Boar', *The Sun*, 1 July 2006, p. 7
10 See homepage of P. Trotter; http://hometown.aol.com/pttrotter/myhomepage/pet.html

the recipient of an Animal Hall of Fame Award for Bravery from the local Arizona Pet Hall of Fame.

GHOSTLY DOG?

Jane Glanville wrote to me about a time when she was in her twenties and used to go out clubbing in Plymouth and then walk home alone in the early hours. One night she was crossing over a footbridge near her house when a man approached her. He did not speak, but walked up close beside her. Suddenly, a huge white dog appeared and walked in between her and the man. As Jane wrote, 'he was very friendly and I patted him on the head. He seemed to be a breed, which I think is called a Pyrenean Mountain Dog. Anyway, he walked along the pavement next to me until I put my key in the front door and got in safely. I turned around to see him but he had gone! Since then, I have become a Christian and wonder if that dog had been sent to protect me from that man?'

PROTECTIVE DOLPHINS

In 1989, an Australian teenager, Adam, and his two friends were surfing in the Pacific Ocean with a school of dolphins. They were all enjoying themselves until suddenly the dolphins started zooming around and under the boys, then surfacing and splashing violently. Something was wrong and the boys were worried.

Just then, Adam saw a fin coming toward him, but it wasn't a dolphin: it was a Tiger Shark! The shark attacked, taking a huge chunk out of Adam's surfboard and knocking him into the water. Adam was wounded. The shark saw him in the water, turned and attacked again. But then the dolphins went after the shark and worked together to chase him away. Adam's human friends helped him to shore. He had bites on his hip, thigh and stomach, but thanks to the dolphins, he lived.[11]

BEN'S MESSAGE IN A BOTTLE

Robert Sinclair has asthma. After a very bad attack, he collapsed in his room and couldn't move. He was unable to go and get help, or eat, or drink. Instead, he lay there for a whole week and became very ill. He decided he had to get help and so he wrote a note, put it in a bottle and dropped it out of his window, hoping that someone would find it and help him. Then he waited.

And someone did find it: Ben! But Ben isn't a person – he's a very intelligent Border Collie dog. Ben picked up the bottle in his mouth and took it home to his human friend, Brian. Once Brian had read the note, he rushed to find Robert. He also called an ambulance, which came and took Robert to hospital. Robert got better, thanks to Ben. He will never forget the amazing dog who saved his life.[12]

DANIEL'S PUMA

Daniel Olin was eleven years old when his parents moved to Edmonton, in Canada. He liked his new school and made friends there, but then things at home started to change. His parents began to argue and the arguments got worse and worse until one day, Daniel's mother left. With his father working long hours, Daniel felt very alone and very unhappy. He wanted to run away and eventually did so.

11 http://www.bodyandmind.co.za/animalcentre/Dolphin_Saves_Lives.html
12 http://www.bodyandmind.co.za/animalcentre/Super_Sheepdog.html

Very early one bitterly cold morning, when the snow was deep on the ground, he packed a bag with some clothes, his Walkman, some chocolate and a map of Canada, and set off. He ran and ran until he was out of breath. His feet were heavy with the snow but he staggered on through deep snowdrifts, not even watching where he was going.

Then, disaster struck. A rock hidden by the deep snow caught his ankle and Daniel fell to the ground, crying in pain. He had broken a bone and no one knew where he was to help him. He was bitterly cold and starting to feel tired, but he knew that if he fell asleep in the snow, he would almost certainly die from hypothermia. A spruce tree stirred ahead. From within the branches, a pair of yellow eyes watched Daniel: a puma had been stalking him. Pumas can be viciously powerful, with claws that could shred Daniel into strips. But instead of moving in for the kill, the Puma approached Daniel and lay across his chest and limbs. Daniel was too frightened to move, but soon the warmth of the animal reached him and he began to feel better. From time to time, the Puma pressed his muzzle against Daniel and rocked his head gently. Clearly, the creature knew that Daniel must not fall asleep. This animal should have been a real danger to Daniel and yet the boy began to feel safe. They remained like that for several hours until Daniel and the Puma heard voices and the rescue team found them.[13]

DOG IN THE SNOW

On Boxing Day in 2003, the Dudleys had been invited to lunch at their daughter's house, so before they set off, they decided to take Josh, their Collie, for a walk. It was late

13 http://www.bodyandmind.co.za/animalcentre/A_Caring_Puma.html

morning and there was a lot of traffic – which Josh hates – and there was a dusting of snow over the icy lanes. Later, Mrs Dudley told her husband how Josh had tugged him back home braving the traffic on his own. Mr Dudley has no recollection of any of this, for he had slipped on ice and needed an ambulance and ten stitches in his head. 'Josh, still on his lead, had led me across the road, up our drive and into our garage – I was not conscious of this happening until rejoining Josh at my daughter's house some four hours later... it could have been much worse if Josh had not been so faithful and clever.'

RESCUE PIG!

When her daughter was called out of town on business, JoAnn offered to watch her pet, Lulu, a pot-bellied pig. Home alone, JoAnn had a major heart attack. She called for help, but no one heard her cries. Lulu sensed JoAnn's predicament and ran out of the house through a small dog door. The pig lay down in the street in an attempt to stop traffic. Periodically, Lulu would return to the house to check on JoAnn and then return to the street in search of assistance. Finally, someone stopped and followed Lulu to the door. The good Samaritan called 911, and JoAnn was rushed to the hospital. Without Lulu's help, she might not be here today.[14]

LIFESAVING HEARING DOGS

Keri is a beautiful, five-year-old Spaniel cross and a working Hearing Dog for profoundly deaf Mel Smith. In addition to her deafness, she also has multiple sclerosis, and Keri has had a

14 http://www.bodyandmind.co.za/animalcentre/Playing_Dead.html

very positive therapeutic effect on Mel, helping her through the bad times. However, recently Keri has also saved Mel from a disastrous situation, as she explains:

'Keri enriches and betters my life, each and every day. Before she came to live with me, I went through a difficult time struggling to cope with having both progressive hearing loss and multiple sclerosis. I often felt pretty sorry for myself and quite alone, and over time, my confidence diminished greatly. In effect, I became a shadow of the person I was before.

'Then, "blue skies". Along came Keri, arriving in my life in 2001 and how much better everything has seemed since then. With the constant love and support I receive from my beautiful, faithful little dog, I feel far more able to attempt new experiences and challenges, knowing she is there for me. The constant contact I have with other people whom I meet through Keri has helped me to cope much better with my deafness in that I can be more positive and upbeat about it: the days when I avoided conversations for fear of not hearing and feeling a fool seem so long ago now.

'Keri really is a perfect partner, and my best friend. In fact, she has many qualities and attributes that are often hard to come by in human partners/friends, i.e. she is extremely loyal and protective, and I know that I am important to her and really believe she would do everything in her power to look out for me and keep me safe. She is non-judgemental, in that she sees everything and everyone at face value, accepting people for who they are with no preconceived ideas. She is both loving and giving – she really wants to please and makes clear her affections, be it with her ever wagging tail, smiley face or loving gaze, and she asks for so little in return. She is compassionate – she knows how to cheer up someone's day and picks up when a lick of the hand is needed to lift spirits – which has been particularly therapeutic to the elderly people we visit through our voluntary work; and lastly, she is committed, both to me and to the vitally important working role she undertakes of being my 'ears', a job she does so well, 100 per cent of the time.

'On top of all this, she recently saved my life. My friends and I, plus Keri, were enjoying a week-long caravan holiday. On this occasion, only Keri and I were present and in my wisdom I decided to light the gas fire.

'I then went into the kitchen to prepare the evening meal. Moments later, I felt a dull thud at the back of my knees and turned to find Keri giving the sign for "danger/emergency", touching with her paws and lying still on the floor. I asked her "What is it?" and again she repeated this action.

'As we were positioned near the smoke alarm, which was not making a sound, I was momentarily tempted to ignore Keri's actions but then I glanced to the lounge area and, to my horror, saw a large flame roaring out of the grill on the gas fire into the room. Before my eyes the fire surround began to bubble and burn, with flames licking around the whole fire, which threatened to set the carpet and wall covering alight. Throughout all of this the smoke alarm remained silent.

180

'I tried unsuccessfully to get the fire extinguisher off the wall, all the while Keri continually touched me and lay down in the danger position. I then ran for help and was accompanied back to the caravan by three people who managed between them to bring the fire under control. On re-entering the caravan, Keri appeared uneasy and began to alert not only me but the others present – running between us and touching and laying down.

'In the end the fire was brought under control, but the whole incident was really shocking and scary, and actually resulted in the caravan being condemned.

'I feel incredibly proud of Keri, because if it wasn't for her actions and persistence, the situation could have been so much worse, life-threatening even. Keri clearly assessed that something was wrong, even though there was no alert sound from the smoke alarm, and was persistent in her efforts to warn me and keep me safe. She definitely seemed concerned when we re-entered the caravan and I believe she alerted the other people because I, in effect, was ignoring her warnings by remaining in the danger area.

'When I explained to our helpers what Keri was doing, they were astounded by how clever she is in being able to adapt her training accordingly and, needless to say, she received lots of fuss and praise.

'I feel indebted to Keri for what she did that day, acting above and beyond her training to keep me safe and in my eyes she truly is a real little hero.'

Bentley is a Norfolk terrier cross and is now nine years old. He was donated to Hearing Dogs for Deaf People and has been an exemplary Hearing Dog for his deaf owner, Colin James, for many years.

However, Bentley's life-saving actions do not apply only to dogs. In addition to his deafness, Colin also suffers from vertigo and a couple of years ago he had a vertigo attack and collapsed while he was in the garden. Immediately, Bentley, who had been with Colin, raced into the house to find Colin's wife Barbara. He alerted her with his paws and then took her back to where Colin lay. Bentley's prompt actions prevented a more serious outcome.

Even more amazing than that is Bentley's most recent heroic act that did, quite literally, save Colin's life. In June 2004, Colin had a minor stroke and, for several months before he could have a pacemaker fitted, his heart would stop at irregular intervals during the night when he was asleep. As a result of this, Barbara was constantly aware that she would need to keep awake to make sure he was still breathing and, if he stopped, she would have to push him to make him start again.

Although Barbara did her best to stay awake to ensure she could nudge Colin, one night she fell asleep. She was woken by Bentley, who had gone round to her side of the bed and touched her to wake her up. She realised Colin had stopped breathing and she pushed him to get him started again. This happened again on a different occasion. On a particularly bad night after the ambulance crew had come and settled Colin back to sleep, Barbara knew she would not sleep again, so at 5am, she went to sit in the lounge but was ready to check on Colin at regular intervals. She need not have worried – just half an hour later, Bentley came to find her, touched her and took her back to the bedroom, where once again Colin had stopped breathing.

All of this is even more remarkable because Bentley is Colin's Hearing Dog and has been trained predominantly to alert Colin, not Barbara to sounds. On these occasions, he was also using his initiative and sixth sense to let Barbara know something was wrong, as he was not actually responding to sounds. Colin has now had a pacemaker fitted and all three can get a decent night's sleep!

Bertie, an eight-year-old Miniature Yorkshire Terrier, has been with his profoundly deaf owner, Gill Stevenson, for nearly six years. He has a gorgeous personality: full of *joie de vivre*, mischievous and very loving, he loves attention and a bit of fuss. However, although he is small, he has made a huge impact on Gill's life, and has potentially saved not only her life, but also that of a stranger.

Gill takes up the story of just how much Bertie has done for her:

'Before I had Bertie I was in the pits of depression and never went out; in fact, I rarely got up in the mornings. I certainly didn't go out for walks, and was reluctant to meet people and chat to complete strangers. When I lost my hearing, I became very isolated and didn't even visit friends and neighbours because I couldn't hold conversations with them. Having Bertie to look after changed all that: it meant I had to go out walking every day, and of course I would meet people and stop to chat, often about Bertie himself. It happens to this day. I have had a long battle to overcome my depression, but I would never have done it without Bertie's help. I was suicidal before I had him – he has literally saved my life.

183

'He has also saved someone else's life. I was in University Hospital in Cardiff for five days in 2001 after an operation. My husband Martin and Bertie were staying nearby and both visited me for as long as possible every day. I missed looking after Bertie and was concerned that he was missing me; he certainly looked forward to seeing me every day, and pulled at the lead as my husband approached along the corridor.

'He had visited me every day before the day of the incident and his behaviour was impeccable. He was allowed to curl up at my feet on the bed, where he stayed, quiet as a mouse, while Martin and I talked. The lady he saved was not elderly – I would say she was only in her forties, but she kept herself to herself. However, the first time she saw Bertie she was over the moon – she made a huge effort to come over to my bed and make a fuss of him, which of course he enjoyed.

'The incident happened in this way: Martin and Bertie were visiting, in the usual way, with Martin sitting at my side talking and Bertie curled up on the bed at my feet. All of a sudden, Bertie stood up and became quite agitated, and Martin told me he was barking. This was totally abnormal behaviour – he rarely barked, he was always quiet as a mouse and very placid – but he was obviously very disturbed by something. He had never reacted in this way before.

'At first I was embarrassed about him being so naughty – I was surprised that he was barking and causing such a commotion, and I was worried that the nurses would ask him to leave. The nurses were all outside the ward, but one came running in. Bertie didn't run over to the lady; he simply kept barking and looking at her, then turning around to look at me to get my attention. I think Martin and I both realised that he was barking at the lady, and Martin stood up and I sat up just as the nurse came in to see what the problem was.

'We told her that Bertie was barking at the lady and asked if she was all right, and because we were expressing concern the nurse went over to check on her. The next thing we knew, she was pressing the emergency button and other nurses rushed in with some equipment, which they used to revive the woman.

'Once she had received attention, Bertie just sat back down on the bed as though nothing had happened! But of course he got a huge fuss from us and from the nurses when they realised what had happened. It appears that her oxygen level had dropped to such a level that she had become unconscious.

'I feel amazed at what Bertie did. He must have some amazing sixth sense or something, or maybe he realised that her breathing was abnormal, but how he could hear her across the ward, I do not know. It certainly does make me feel more secure, knowing that if I was in trouble, Bertie would probably realise and alert someone.

'I can sum up Bertie in one word – lifesaver. Not just because he saved this lady's life in the hospital, but because he has saved mine, too.'

June Beech is profoundly deaf and Valentine is her first hearing dog. They have been together for over five years. Valentine is a six-and-a-half-year-old mongrel who was

donated to Hearing Dogs and, according to June, she is a
paramedic, wonderdog and guardian angel all in one. When
June first had Valentine, she alerted her to the fact that her
father-in-law had fallen in the bedroom between the bed and
the wall as he had had a stroke. June had been out in the
garden and had not heard anything, but Valentine realised
something was wrong and, even though she had not been
given a command, she ran to fetch June and took her back
to where he was lying. He was later admitted to hospital.

Then Valentine became quite ill and was admitted to
the vet's hospital with viral enteritis and was on a drip.
June was told that she nearly lost her. Nevertheless, she
came through it, and after three days June brought her
home but was told not to work her, which she didn't.

June takes up the story:

'One day, my husband went out to the garage. It was
raining and I was in the kitchen preparing the vegetables.
Valentine started touching me, but I ignored her saying,
"No, the vet said no titbits." She went away and I
turned back to the sink.

'All of a sudden Valentine came flying at my legs and
suddenly I knew that she wanted me to follow. She took
me to the patio doors, where I found my husband collapsed
on the patio in the pouring rain. My husband was
admitted to hospital with a suspected brain haemorrhage.

'Another time Valentine was a paramedic was when
my grandson was about two and was playing out on the
patio at home when a strong gust of wind blew him into
a bush. Before my grandson started to cry, or before we

even knew about it, Valentine was up and ran to him and was comforting him.

'Again, Valentine acted above and beyond her training when she came to my aid when we were out. I was walking up the high street and was going to cross a very busy road. I went to cross the road, in between two parked lorries. I looked and said to Valentine, "It's all right we can go." Valentine would not cross, but kept backing towards the pavement. All of a sudden, I looked up and there was a lorry passing at speed. I realised that I would have been underneath that lorry. Since then, Valentine will only let me cross on a pedestrian crossing.

'Due to my hearing loss I lose my balance and fall over quite frequently. Recently, Valentine came to my aid when I got up in the early hours when it was quite dark and I failed to put the light on. Coming back from the bathroom, I lost my balance and fell. Valentine came rushing out of the bedroom to see if I was all right. I said to her that I was OK before she would settle down in her sleeping position beside my bed.

'Valentine is indeed a very heroic Hearing Dog, very kind and very loving to everyone she meets. To me, Valentine is not just my working dog but a very dear friend as well, and we work as one.'

ANIMALS FINDING INJURED PEOPLE

Annette adopted Norman, a blind yellow Labrador, from the pound. The beach is the only place he can run free because he is blind. One day, as Annette and Norman were walking along the beach, Norman cocked his ear and took off running. He heard something no one else could hear – the cries of someone in trouble. Lisa, fifteen, had been swimming with her brother and got caught in the current. Norman swam towards her cries and, with Annette's voice guiding him, pulled Lisa back to shore. Lisa considers Norman her guardian angel.[15]

A similar incident happened amid a heavy blizzard with 60 cm of snow, but this time it involved a horse called China and sixty-four-year-old Mrs Sergeant and her eighteen-month-old dog Zoe, a Lhasa Apso. The small dogs are originally from Tibet and known for their keen intelligence and excellent hearing. As she did every morning, Mrs Sergeant walked from her house to exercise Zoe on the Gosbeck's Archaeological Park. She walked through the gap in the fence at the back of her garden, over a stile to the bridlepath which skirts the site.

It was cold, wintry and bright, and Mrs Sergeant was extremely wary of slipping so she decided she would be more certain of her footing if she walked closer to the hedgerow that was running to her left as the snow was less deep there and posed less of a risk. Moments after leaving the path, her foot disappeared down a fox hole and, with her leg stuck down the hole up to her knee, she fell. She tried to move her foot and then the pain kicked in. 'I've never experienced pain like it before and knew I would not be able to walk on it,' she said. It appeared that a piece of bone had splintered off her tibia just under her knee!

The following hour passed without incident – Mrs Sergeant was not worried as she was sure someone would come down the path, find her and get help. But no one did. She was getting

15 http://www.bodyandmind.co.za/animalcentre/Cry_for_Help.html

colder and no one could hear her cries as the wind whipped around her.

Meanwhile, Errol, who owned the land nearby, had turned his horse China out into the field as he mucked the stable out and threw him some hay to graze on. Usually, China would have eaten his breakfast quietly, then waited to be saddled, but that morning he kept racing to Errol and then charging down the field and galloping around the fence. Errol just thought he had been spooked by the wind, so carried on mucking out, but when he had finished China was still very agitated. As Errol said, 'I knew something was wrong. I looked at him, he looked at me and I followed him to the corner of the paddock.'

From the far end of the paddock, he realised what had caught China's attention – he could distinctly hear Mrs Sergeant's calls for help. Realising how bleak the conditions were, Errol got back-up help from Martin, who was close by on his tractor, and the two men made their way through the snow to the hedgerow separating the paddock from the bridleway, forcing their way through. Hidden low down in the hedge was Mrs Sergeant – she was still conscious but needed warmth, and urgently. 'Her lips were already blue and she was white and freezing cold,' recalled Errol. Fearing the onset of hypothermia, Errol called an ambulance, redirecting it a second time to the best point of access to the bridleway.

It was only later that Mrs Sergeant was told that her saviour was currently calmly eating hay in his paddock. 'There's no doubt about it,' says Errol, 'if China hadn't have acted like he did that morning, I would never have known she was there.'

The twist in this story, though, was that Mrs Sergeant was unaware that that very morning China's owner, show-jumping enthusiast Errol Flynn had called the vet out to discuss China's arthritis and whether it might be better to put Chine to sleep. Errol could not bear to say goodbye to his trusty friend of sixteen years and believed him still to have some quality years in him yet. It was that decision hours earlier which had indeed saved Mrs Sergeant.

ANIMALS HELPING THEIR OWN

Twycross Zoo wrote to tell me about their Bonobo 'Kuni', a type of Chimpanzee who 'rescued' a starling that had flown into the bonobo enclosure. Kuni managed to prevent the frightened bird from being caught by the other Bonobos and then holding it in his cupped hands, he climbed to the top of the tallest tree in the enclosure, spread the starling's wings out and released it to freedom. This was seen by Betty Walsh, and even got a mention in Frans de Waal's book, *Bonobo, The Forgotten Ape*.[16]

SCAMPY AND SIMON

Scampy has been a working Hearing Dog for over eight years, but when she first came to live with her deaf owner, June, she had to get used to June's cat Simon, too! Fortunately for Scampy, Simon warmed to her straightaway – mainly because of the attention that Scampy gave him, especially in the mornings when she would lick him on the cheek to wake him.

Their close bond was demonstrated when Scampy saved Simon's life. One evening, Scampy and June had gone up to

16 Cumming, Tess, & Wolstencraft, David, *Pet Power*, Ebury Press, London pp. 32–7.

bed, and Simon followed, but after a while he went back downstairs. Shortly afterwards, just as June was dropping off to sleep, Scampy rushed over to her bedside and kept touching June with her paw, which was her way of alerting her to a sound. Scampy then rushed downstairs in a panic, and June followed her knowing, that something was very wrong. She suddenly saw what Scampy was staring at: Simon had caught himself on a cord that was hanging on the banisters and it was wound tightly round his neck. In trying to free himself, it had tightened so much he was beginning to choke to death. If Scampy had not alerted June as quickly as she did, there is no doubt that Simon would have died.

BENTLEY SAVES POACHER

Bentley, a Norfolk Terrier cross, was donated to Hearing Dogs for Deaf People and has been an exemplary Hearing Dog with his life-saving actions not confined to helping his owner Colin James. The first incident happened a few years ago when Bentley was playing outside in the garden with Colin's elderly pet dog, Poacher. Colin was inside when Bentley suddenly rushed in to find him, alerted him with his paws, then led him out into the garden. Colin discovered Poacher choking and immediately rushed her to the vet, who found that a piece of food had got stuck in her throat. If Bentley had not been quite so quick, Poacher would have choked to death. From dogs to horses, pumas to pigs, animals don't only look after themselves, but humans as well.

CHAPTER 9

Special Celebrity Animals

Here, Gentlemen, a dog teaches us a lesson in humanity.
NAPOLEON BONAPARTE

Animals have been entertaining film and television viewers for years. Even in ancient times, there is evidence that the Greek author Plutarch wrote about a Poodle-like dog named Zoppico, who performed for the Emperor Vespasian over 2,000 years ago. Zoppico's famous trick of 'playing dead' was to eat a piece of meat and fall over as if he were dead, but he would be miraculously revived by the audience's applause. The natural ability many animals have to learn tricks and interact with human actors has touched countless theatre audiences' and moviegoers' lives. Dogs in particular are receptive to learning complex instructions and can then draw on their own personalities to make their mark on a role. Bringing happiness to millions of people may not seem as remarkable as some of the more heroic feats covered earlier, but having witnessed the positive effects of human-animal interaction, the work of special celebrity animals is not to be underestimated.

Today, animals have become as famous as film stars, supermodels, politicians and singers, becoming spokespersons for products, services and campaigns. If put in a poll, the most respected animal from the big screen would most probably be Rin Tin Tin, the German Shepherd who became the first animal star in Hollywood.

RIN TIN TIN

At the end of World War I Corporal Lee Duncan stumbled upon an abandoned German war dog station containing a mother German Shepherd and her five pups. Being an animal lover he rescued the shivering canines. When he was discharged he took two of the puppies back to the U.S.A. He called them Nanette and Rin-Tin-Tin. Unfortunately Nanette contracted pneumonia and died. Rin-Tin-Tin went on to become a famous movie star.

Rin Tin Tin made his debut in *The Man From Hell's River* in 1922. Warner Brothers snapped up the charismatic canine in 1923. He earned $1,000 a week, was insured for $100,000, had his own production unit, limo and chauffeur, his own orchestra for mood music, wore a diamond-studded collar and was served steak prepared by his own chef! The talented German Shepherd signed his own contracts (with a paw print) and for a time was his studio's biggest star. He starred in twenty-four films, the success of which kept the studio afloat, and also had the effect of saving many neighbourhood movie houses from closure.

'Rinty' (as he was nicknamed) performed all his own superstunts. He could remain in a stay position for up to 30 minutes at a time and knew how to play to the camera as well as any human star. The movie mogul Darryl F. Zanuck was responsible for several of Rinty's scripts before he himself became famous.

Rinty was a one-man dog and bonded with Lee Duncan in a special way. His highly-strung nature was kept in check by love for his trainer. He could be unpredictable and more than one co-star came away with a nip or two.

The love life of any superstar is always of great interest to their adoring public and, when eligible bachelor Rinty was paired with a female German Shepherd, the 'wedding' made all the papers. They appeared together in a few films and eventually produced Rin Tin Tin Junior, who also went on to make a little career for himself in the movies.

Rinty's last film was *Rough Waters* in 1930. When the studio released him he made two low-budget serials before enjoying a happy but short-lived retirement. In 1932, at the age of fourteen, he died suddenly while playing with his beloved master. Neighbour and animal lover, the actress Jean Harlow ran over to help but nothing could be done, and Duncan cradled Rinty and wept.[1]

Since Rin Tin Tin, we've been amused and entertained by countless animals, from cats and dogs, to whales and horses. Celebrity animals are veterans of the media spotlight, always

1 Information taken from *The Silents Majority* by Diane MacIntyre 1996/7

ready to entertain. Even though a celebrity pet's payoff isn't a Hollywood mansion and a busty starlet, they are consummate pros. They sell the product, convey the message, save the boy trapped in the well, get the job done. In death, celebrity animals are often remembered better than their human counterparts. America even boasts a grave tour (http://www.roadsideamerica.com/pet/ladadog.html) that fans can follow to visit the graves and memorials of some of our best-loved celebrity animals from Flipper to Martha the Passenger Pigeon, to Leo the MGM Lion.

Volney Phifer was Hollywood's premier animal trainer and he knew better than any one how to make an animal sit up and pay attention. One of his most successful protégés was Leo, the MGM lion, who he taught to roar on cue.

By the 1930s, Volney had made his fortune and left Tinseltown to buy a farm in Gillette, New Jersey, where he boarded animals used in Broadway shows and Manhattan vaudeville acts. He brought Leo with him, and here is where both man and beast died. Volney planted Leo in the front yard and marked the grave with a small, blank block of granite. More significant is the pine tree that Volney planted directly over Leo's body. Volney was very much in touch with his European ancestry and insisted the tree's roots would 'hold down the lion's spirit'.

LASSIE

Next up in the line of celebrity dogs must be Lassie, with a grand total of 53 years on TV, and a UK remake of *Lassie Come Home* released in 2005.

Rudd Weatherwax got Pal (later to be Lassie) as a payment for a debt. The actor and animal trainer ran a kennel and supplied movie dogs but he also taught regular obedience. Pal chased motorcycles and his owner sent him to be trained but then decided he did not want him back! Rudd took Pal on, curing all his behavioural problems but never did stop him from chasing motorcycles.

Around 1942, *Lassie Come Home* went into production with a female collie hired to play the lead. Pal had previously auditioned for the part but was turned down because he was not a show Collie. Rudd went home and began training Pal to do all the trademark Lassie tricks, feeding him a special diet to bring out his coat. He auditioned for the part yet again and yet again was turned down but this time offered a role as a stunt dog.

The script called for the lead dog to swim across a raging river, but the female show Collie would not go near the water. Now Pal got his chance! He jumped into the river, swam desperately to the other side, dragged himself out and collapsed. There was not a dry eye in the house. The director was so impressed, he said, 'Pal may have gone into the water but Lassie has come out.' All the dogs portraying Lassie have been male. Females are usually 10–15 lbs lighter and Lassie needs to be a big, heroic dog with a thicker coat. Female Collies were not ignored because they are any less intelligent – in fact, some of Lassie's own stunt doubles have been female. Pal went on to be the first in a long line of Weatherwax-bred and trained Lassies spanning over 50 years, bringing comfort and joy to characters and moviegoers alike, who delight in the dog's ability to sense danger and communicate, changing human lives for the better.

TOTO

From start to finish, Toto plays a very important role in MGM's classic film, *The Wizard of Oz* (1939). Toto was a Cairn Terrier whose real name was Terry, even though Toto was referred to as 'he' in the movie, the Cairn was really a 'she'.

Aljean Harmetz points out in her book, *The Making of The Wizard of Oz* (Random House, New York, 1977), that 'It was not a human actor but the dog, Toto, for whom the longest search was made. The Property Department was handed a copy of L. Frank Baum's book and told to find a dog that looked like the one in W.W. Denslow's drawings. No one in the Property Department could recognise the breed Denslow had drawn.' Hollywood animal trainer Carl Spitz acquired Terry, almost four years before the film was made. Believe it or not, as Spitz began training Terry, the dog was so shy that for three weeks she didn't come out from under the bed. Once she had overcome her stage fright, however, Terry – or rather Spitz – received a salary of $125 a week during the filming of *The Wizard of Oz*.

Just like her human co-stars, Terry was not exempt from receiving injuries during filming. Harmetz elaborates in her book as follows: 'It had taken the dog weeks to learn how to cope with the wind machines. Eventually, she had learned to duck behind the principals when the wind machines were turned on. Then, during the rehearsals of the scene where Toto is pursued by the soldiers, one of them jumped on top of her and sprained her foot.'

The role of Toto in L. Frank Baum's 1902 musical version of *The Wizard of Oz* was played by humans as a spotted calf named 'Imogene' rather than a dog. This was before the time of training animals was as commonplace as it is today. In his book, *The Annotated Wizard of Oz* (Crown Publishing, New York, 1976), Michael Patrick Hearn includes Baum's own explanation of his decision to do this. 'We found Toto an impossibility from the dramatic viewpoint, and reluctantly abandoned him. But we put the cow in his place. It may seem a long jump from a dog to a cow, but in the latter animal we have a character that really ought to amuse the youngsters exceedingly, and the eccentric creature accompanies Dorothy on her journey from Kansas, just as Toto did in the book.'

EDDIE

The canine character Eddie, played by feisty Jack Russell terrier Moose, drove Kelsey Grammer's lead character crazy for ten years on the TV comedy *Frasier* and died at the ripe age of sixteen at the Los Angeles home of trainer Mathilde Halberg. It wasn't all acting on Moose's part, though. He was naturally 'extremely mischievous,' Halberg said. His contribution to the show's – and Grammer's – success was publicly noted by the actor when he accepted a 1994 Emmy for best actor in a comedy. 'Most important, Moose, this is for you,' Grammer said, good naturedly. Moose, who also played the older dog Skip in the 2000 film *My Dog Skip*, was retired in recent years. A one-time cover star of *Entertainment Weekly* magazine, Moose had been a rescue dog before his entrée into showbusiness.

KEIKO

You may know him simply as 'that whale from *Free Willy*' but in fact his real name was Keiko, and he has a story to tell. Keiko was born in the Atlantic Ocean, near Iceland in either 1977 or 1978 and was captured when he was around a year old and taken to Saedyrasfnid, an aquarium in Iceland. Three years later, in 1982 he was bought by a theme park and aquarium called Marineland in Ontario, Canada, where he performed before the public. At this point, he began to develop skin lesions on his body.

In 1985 he was sold onto Reino Adventura in Mexico for the comparatively measly sum of $350,000 and he began to perform again. Warner Brothers begin making the first *Free Willy* film in 1992, on location in Mexico, filming Keiko. After the film was released the public leant on Warner Brothers to do something about the living conditions of Keiko after alarming reports in the media relating to the so-called 'inadequate living conditions, and chronic health problems'. With the park's cooperation, Warner Brothers stepped in to find Keiko a better place to live. The groundswell of popular support for Keiko was understandable. Yet again, people who had seen a film in which a mammalian character relies on their intuition and perception to communicate with a human, as well as responding positively to training and filming, felt a special connection. With the help of the Earth Island Institute, an aquarium in Newport, Oregon, was prepared to take Keiko on. The aquarium filled all the critical criteria, such as 'no performing, cold clean sea water, and room to accommodate the huge pool to be built for Keiko.

In 1994 the Keiko Foundation was formed. With Warner Brothers donating an initial $4 million, the mission was to rehabilitate Keiko in a new home and then on to his possible release back into the wild. The very next year, the Keiko Foundation and the Mexican Park jointly announced that Keiko would be moved to the Oregon Coast Aquarium. The cost of the new pool being built for him was $7.3 million. School children around the world began to hold fundraising events to help the Keiko Foundation look after Keiko.

Keiko's move from Mexico to Oregon went ahead as planned in January 1996. Still a big star in Mexico, many families visited Keiko for the last time to say goodbye. He arrived at Newport Municipal Airport and was introduced to his new home. By the end of 1996 he had gained more than 1,000 pounds in weight and his skin lesions were beginning to decrease.

In 1997 live fish were placed in Keiko's tank, in order to encourage him to start hunting again. At first he wasn't interested, but after three weeks he had caught and eaten at least one black cod by himself. He was not given live fish again until the beginning of 1998.

In January 1998, lesion-free and after two months of medical examinations, Keiko was given a clean bill of health. By April 1998 he was managing to hunt, kill and eat live Steelhead trout, eating up to half his daily food intake in this way. Eventually he swam from Iceland to Norway, where he became so popular that he was moved to a more remote fjord, where he died aged 27.

FAMOUS AROUND THE WORLD

It's not just in the entertainment industry where famous animals have impressed with their ability to change our lives. Ham was the world's first 'astrochimp', and the first free creature in outer space, long before Laika was sent up in Sputnik 2 by the Russians. He blasted off from Cape Canaveral on 31 January 1961, and travelled 155 miles (250km) in 16.5 minutes before landing safely in the Atlantic. The first American human to orbit the earth, John Glenn, was rewarded with a seat in the US Senate. Ham's reward was simply an apple!

After his space mission, Ham lived in the National Zoo in Washington, DC, for seventeen years. Fretting animal activists, who had not underestimated Ham's good work, worried that he languished there, a lonely superstar with a single tyre hanging from his ceiling. So, in 1981, Ham was moved to a zoo in North Carolina. There, he socialised with other chimps and found a special lady chimp to love. He died peacefully of old age in 1983, aged 27. His' body was shipped west, and is buried in the front lawn of the International Space Hall of Fame in Alamogordo, New Mexico.

Dying of distemper, Radar was found in a kennel in Brazil in 1960. As a result of careful nursing and care he survived and became a TV personality. On coming to England, he appeared on *The David Frost Show* and then became a famous face in the police drama, *Softly Softly* where he played the part of a police dog with TV handler P.C. Snow, a part played by Terrence Rigby. His career was distinguished and he attracted a huge following.

CHAPTER 10

Animal After-Death Communication

'Lots of people talk to animals, not very many listen, though – that's the problem.'

BENJAMIN HOFF, THE TAO OF POOH

PET DEATH

Recently, people's attitude to the death of a pet has changed radically, with burial ceremonies becoming an important part of the relationship.

The belief that dogs can see spirits and apparitions while having the ability to sense that death is near is not new. In the history books, two such circumstances are well documented and involve the explorer Howard Carter and Lord Carnarvon, who financed the discovery of Tutankhamen's tomb; a tomb that was supposed to have a curse placed upon it, which was directed towards anyone who violated that tomb. When Lord Carnarvon became ill and died in 1923, it is reported that his faithful dog also died within a few hours of his master's demise. Similarly, it is said that just before Abraham Lincoln was assassinated his dog started howling and running wildly round the White House.

In today's society, animal death and pet bereavement is reported widley, with pet cemeteries and pet crematoria in Britain now commonplace, frequently hitting the headlines with their newsworthy combination of meeting a real need and sentimentalising the death of an animal.[1] The Cambridge Pet Crematorium and Cemetery, for example, featured as a major story in the *Radio Times* [2].

In the early 1990s Professor Douglas Davies carried out a UK survey in which he explored pet death[3], and upon asking the question, 'Do you think animals have souls?' a staggering 77 per cent said yes, they did, 6 per cent said no, while 15 per cent said they didn't know.

Some human-animal relationships are, in fact, profound, leaving the owners just as bereaved as when a member of their family dies; some more so. After all, a pet is there twenty-four hours a day, seven days a week by your side, so to have it suddenly taken away from you can often leave more of a void and a sense of loss in some ways than the loss of a relative would.

1 Davies, D., *Death, Ritual and Belief*, p. 168, Cassell, London, 1997

2 *Radio Times*, 27 April 1991, with an extensive documentary

3 For detailed results and analysis of this survey, see Davies, D., *Death, Ritual and Belief*, pp. 169–72, Cassell, London, 1997

ANIMAL AFTER-DEATH COMMUNICATION

My second book, *After-Death Communication*, focused on humans receiving spontaneous and unaided messages from the other side, and while wading through letters and testimonies there was an amount describing special dreams, visions, scents, or experiences involving beloved pets who had passed over, which could not be ignored.

This leads us to the great question of the existence of animal souls, which has been debated in theological circles for centuries. Although it is too vast a topic to venture into here, I will surmise by saying that there is no shortage of supporters of the view that animals do have souls. Hippocrates stated that 'the soul is the same in all living creatures, although the body of each is different', and Pythagorus also claimed that 'animals share with us the privilege of having a soul', and more recently thousands of veterinary surgeons have reached the same conclusion.

From my own experience, while writing *Seeing Angels*, I encountered many stories which mentioned animals being there at the time of the experience – most picked up on something being in the room. In the case of being present when a human died, the animals often expressed terror, 'as if they'd seen a ghost'. More interestingly, the accounts sent to me for *After-Death Communication*, with details of deceased animals returning from the grave, were in such number that an entire chapter was dedicated to it, and it has been on my mind a lot while writing this book, which is why it is worthwhile looking at the topic again here.

REINCARNATED PETS

The topic of reincarnation is too vast to touch on in any shape or form here, so I will merely report accounts that suggest it could be possible. Madeleine's dog, Ace, died in June 2006 and she believes he has returned in the form of their new puppy Kachina.

'When she died, Ace had a teat missing from her tummy and another out of place. This was from surgery to remove a tumour.[4] It turned out that Kachina was born with the same features – a missing teat and one that did not match its opposing partner!

Madeleine also received a letter from Margaret Fozzard in Wakefield, who had a kitten called Puska after their cat Jed had died two years before. She was not planning on having another cat but their daughter had taken a friend to choose a kitten and when they took him round to show her parents, Puska just launched himself at Margaret refusing to let go, crying and clinging to her, so she had no choice but to keep him – he was there to stay! As Margaret wrote, 'at just ten weeks,' Puska worked the cat flap, watched TV just like Jed, and stood up like a meerkat to wash himself, just like Jed used to do. Even stranger, our other cats just accepted him immediately, as if they already knew him![5]

PETS RETURN

As discussed in the introduction, the bonds and the importance and significance placed on pets by their owners

4 *Chat It's Fate!* Magazine, August/September issue
5 *Chat It's Fate!* Magazine, August/September issue, 'Dear Madeleine' page.

mean that it is not that hard for non-pet owners to grasp the sense of grief the pet's death brings and the fact that animal afterlife is seen as a natural progression to the beliefs surrounding a human afterlife.

Barbara Gilbert's letter was the first I opened when writing *After Death Communication*. It began: 'My story is not about a human, but my beloved dog who died nine years ago last September ...' Without thinking, I put it to one side. However, slowly the pile became higher as more letters outlined tales of deceased pets. I had not asked specifically for accounts of people seeing pets return, but there were so many, I thought that this warranted further investigation.

Barbara's letter continued:

'I came home from work on New Year's Eve about three months after my dog had passed away. I was looking out of my kitchen window and I saw my beloved Reuben (he was a Red Boxer) in the garden. I could not believe my eyes. The next day Reuben's partner, our other Boxer, became ill and we had to have her put to sleep a few days later... it was as though he had returned to come and wait for her...

'Years after this, another boxer of ours died in my arms – she had a bad heart. As she was passing over, I was sending up healing prayers for her and I saw her spirit leave her body. The only way I can describe it is it looked like a white butterfly with its wings closed. One night last year I was in bed watching TV – it was late so it was dark and I saw a white butterfly outside my bedroom window –

I really think it was that dog who had come to let me know she was alright. I have told several mediums about her passing and they all have told me how lucky I am to have had such a wonderful experience.'

In her book, *Pathway To The Spirit World* (First American Publishing, Madison, 1995), Hashi-Hanta discusses her poodle, Chum Boy, dying when she was away from home. However, he returned to visit twice her to say goodbye. Wide awake, she saw him run into her bedroom and jump up onto her bed and into her arms. She held him briefly both times and noticed that he was younger and fully restored to health. Another example of this occurrence is from Val Baker, who wrote:

'When I lived in Somerset, we went to the RSPCA and came back with a sixth-month-old, black, long-haired cat, whom we called Benson. There were a number of problems with the house we were living in at the time (it was haunted and we had the priest come to cleanse and bless the house) and my relationship with my husband deteriorated. But to cut a long story short, the cat followed me everywhere; he was more like a dog in his behaviour. Whenever I was upset, he would come and sit next to me – he seemed to understand things telepathically.

'He moved with me after my marriage broke up (I got custody) and [my son] Josh, [cat] Benson and myself ended up in Cheltenham. The cat was one of the family and would even sit on a chair at the table when we had family gathering. He would seem to be happy and

content when he knew we were happy and laughing. Everyone who met the cat commented on how unusual he was. Then, at the age of fourteen, his kidneys failed. We administered treatment to prolong his life, but in the end he had to be put to sleep and I was devastated as I had lost a loyal and faithful family member. A couple of weeks after he died, I went to bed and turned out the light. Suddenly, I felt a cat jump on my bed and curl up next to me, just as he had done when he was alive. I put out my hand to the space where I could feel him and to my surprise, I could feel fur! I was very happy about this. After a while, I drifted off to sleep, but as I turned over in the night I heard a thud and realised the ghost cat had fallen off the bed! He then jumped back on to settle down again. I was surprised by this because for some reason, I did not think ghosts would fall off things! He continued to come back and visit me for quite some time and I still think about him, but I have not seen or felt his presence for quite a while.'

One Hilary Price mentioned in passing how she has awoken on several occasions to feel and see her late cat Misty curled up on top of her feet at the bottom of her bed. Each time she has reached out to stroke her, she has 'melted' away. Such an experience is so common. Many people have mentioned seeing deceased animals, albeit briefly, perhaps curled up at the foot of their bed, or in a favourite place on the sofa, or, like Barbara, playing in the garden. Others hear their pets, as did Judy with her eight-month-old pet cat, Magic, who had disappeared.

'About seven to ten days after her disappearance, I awoke to her meowing loudly in my right ear, as she often did when she was hungry and wanted me to get up and feed her. At first, I thought I had been dreaming when I woke up, but I continued to hear the meowing from the living room, which is just off our bedroom. I jumped out of bed screaming, "Magic! Magic!" but I couldn't find her anywhere. I must have spent a good hour looking behind furniture, in other rooms, under the bed and calling her continuously. I was completely baffled but, later, I decided that I must be grieving much more than I had been willing to admit. However, her visits continued … the last one being about five days ago.'

As with sensing deceased relatives, a familiar smell has also been reported on several occasions by owners smelling their beloved animals who have passed on. Both Richard Giles and his friend Andy Weekes smelt the familiar smell of Richard's family dog a good six months after he had passed on.

'For thirteen years, we had a daft Basset Hound dog who was the heart of the family and adored by us all. During the last three years of his life, he suffered liver problems and arthritis, finally taking a turn for the worse and dying in December 2001.

'In the mid-summer of 2002, a friend and I had a strange experience when we arrived home at around 2am. As we entered through the front door, the entire hallway was filled with the warm fuzzy smell of the dog. My friend Andy and I turned to each other and simultaneously said,

"Oh my God, it smells like Droopy." People may assume that it could have been a simple build-up of smells in the carpets and in the furniture, but why would this smell suddenly occur without reason at 2am on a summer's night, and then immediately disappear? It's not logical! Also, the theory of another dog being in the house at the time isn't credible as we have never replaced Droopy. The only conclusion we can draw is that this was a communication from Droopy that we, as humans, are yet to understand.'

NEAR-DEATH EXPERIENCES AND PETS

Now, among near death experiences (NDE), while many people are greeted by a 'being of light', or deceased love ones, some report having been greeted by beloved deceased animals, as did Jackie Jones-Hunt, who had her NDE while in hospital. It involved travelling on a train, and she knew that if she had boarded it she would not have come back:

> *'I had haemorrhaged and that is when my late grandfather and beloved dog came to assist me, and what my grandad said was verified by the doctors! [He had told me I had] a blood clot on a lung and that I needed to sit if I could, to save my life. During the night in hospital, my dog was lying against my right calf, where they found the beginning of a deep vein thrombosis due to the haemorrhage.'*

A rather unusual account was sent to me by Sylvia Hickman about her friend Barbara, who has a serious heart condition with other complications, including high blood pressure. The event involved her cat George, who was one of many strays she had saved, and who was about ten years old. Barbara had always described George as a very ordinary cat, who eats and sleeps but who has no real personality or individual traits to speak of – he was not unaffectionate, but was not a demonstrative cat either.

While doing her household chores one afternoon, Barbara began to feel very tired and exhausted, so decided to sit down for a while in front of the television before returning to her jobs. She remembered watching an old black-and-white film and dozed off into what seemed a deep and restful sleep. She came to, realising she felt freezing cold from head to foot despite the room being quite warm. Barbara looked at the television. All she could see was a brilliant white light and misty clouds, and the outside edge of the television, which was shining a silvery white through the mist. There was no sound. The television was getting smaller and smaller, and appeared to be moving away. She described herself as sinking and thought, 'Is this it? I'm dying?' She felt a great peace and a part of her wanted to go, a part wanted to stay, but she realised she had no control over whatever was happening.

Suddenly she heard a thud. George had leapt from his favourite place, on the top of another armchair, and hit the floor and jumped straight onto her legs. She found him looking directly into her eyes very closely. Then he kept nudging his nose into her face, pushing and pushing hard. She put her arms around him, he felt really warm and the heat filled her 'right down to the toes', she says. She hugged and hugged him, and the room and television returned to normal as she was pulled back. George, totally out of character, fussed and fussed around her for ages.

Did George help save Barbara's life that day? Could George sense she needed him and instinctively did what he did? We will never know. Whatever the answer, it is something which will always remain with Barbara and the odd thing is that she has seen a real difference in him since that occurrence; he tends to follow her about more and has become a much more loving cat. She cannot explain what happened that afternoon but is so grateful that George was there – she has a very different impression of him now!

PETS SENDING OUT MESSAGES FOR HELP AND FINAL GOODBYES

Among numerous accounts of animals communicating with humans, one of a beloved Labrador saying his last farewell to his owners struck me because she reached them at the same time when they were in separate places.

Tara was a large, cream-coloured Labrador. To say she was much loved would be an understatement; the whole family adored her and she was decidedly spoilt. She belonged to the O'Gara family, who found the idea that she was old and failing in health difficult to cope with. Her favourite place was a cosy rug in front of the fire, a spot she chose to lie in more and more, curling up to snooze. One day, the dreadful decision had to be made, as suggested by the local vet, to let Tara go to sleep gently and avoid further pain. John O'Gara was to take her to the vet on the last morning while his wife, Pauline, decided that she would wait at home. Saying goodbye was hard, but Pauline knew that they were doing the very best for Tara.

Sitting in the lounge at 8.50am. with a cup of coffee, Pauline gazed at the spot where Tara would normally be snoozing, wondering if in fact she had already gone to sleep for the last time. The day was dull and overcast, but all at once a bright shaft of light streamed through the window and illuminated the very spot where Tara would have been lying. The light was pure white and emanated a warm feeling of love. Sometime later, John arrived home from the vets, announcing that Tara had closed her eyes and simply drifted away peacefully. 'A very strange thing happened, however,' he said. 'Just as she was going to sleep, a bright shaft of light came through the window of the vet's surgery, shining directly on Tara.' The vet was taken by surprise – the day was so very grey and there was no sun in the sky – 'Where do you suppose that came from?' asked the vet. 'We were baffled,' John added. 'What time would that be?' Pauline asked. 'Well,' John replied, 'it was exactly 8.50am., because I looked at the clock as she closed her eyes.' At that moment, Pauline knew Tara had said goodbye to them both at exactly the same time. 'Tara is safe in the hands of the angels,' Pauline said.[6]

Garth wrote of his experiences with his cats:

'My wife and I had recently had to give permission to our vet to put down our beloved Burmese tomcat, Sam. He was twelve years old, had been suffering from what had originally been diagnosed as chronic kidney deterioration, but during his last couple of days of life, the vet had carried

6 Taken from Eckersley, Glennyce, *An Angel is Forever*

out a biopsy and discovered that Sam had cancer on one of his kidneys. This devastated us because Sam had been a very special animal and we couldn't contemplate the idea of losing communication with him. To understand this, it is necessary for me to digress a little regarding his character and our relationship, which is not so very commonplace between most cat owners and their pets, but tends to be fairly characteristic of owners of Burmese cats, who seem to have something particularly spiritual in their natures, especially their capacity for love.

'I have always believed that part of the responsibility of being a pet owner is to contribute to their evolution by "educating" them as much as possible regarding their environment and life in general. Consequently, from the time Sam was a baby kitten, I had taken him for walks, taken him out in the car, shown him people swimming and boating in the sea (the expression in his eyes was something to see!), taken him to the railway station to see trains with people getting on and off them, played him classical music and showed him pictures in books (he was particularly fascinated by brightly coloured pictures of ancient Egypt and the pyramids!).

'I work at home, essentially alone, although Sam would sit in the chair opposite me while I typed away on the computer, and then at the same time every day when he considered I had been working long enough, he would come over on to my chest and try to get me to stop typing, or else he would just watch the cursor moving over the screen and then work out the connection between the key strokes and the appearance of letters, and watch bemused as pictures would change on the screen and all kinds of inexplicable phenomena that were part of my electronic human experience presented themselves to him. Like most cats, he had adjusted to television and the telephone long ago and took them in his stride.

'Obviously, our relationship had become very, very special over the years. My wife and I were heartbroken as we held him while he was put down. My problem was not so much accepting that we had had to put him out of pain; that was obvious. It was the sense of complete finality, and the feeling that all of that communication I had spent so many years building between us and all that evolutionary progress Sam had made was suddenly for nothing. I couldn't accept easily the inference that there was nothing left of him, that he was just a body. That lively intelligence, the look of love in his eyes and his insistence on expressing every cat opinion in loud stentorian tones and his social graces and cat etiquette, all extinguished in a moment.

'My wife and I both found it very difficult to cope with for many weeks, even though she was convinced that animals had souls which survived death. She believed that Burmese cats' souls would join a kind of group Burmese soul, but I hated the thought that Sam would lose his individuality and become just part of an amorphous mass soul.

'Ten years earlier, we had lost another cat, Tara, who also died of kidney failure. She had been alive when we obtained Sam and upon her death it seemed as though Sam had somehow immediately assimilated many of her personality traits, including the way he played games from that day on, his understanding of the vocabulary we used to talk to him, which had seemed to evoke no response prior to Tara's death, but which he seemed to understand immediately, once she had died. So I had thought that my wife was probably right and that there was a universal Burmese soul into which Sam had been assimilated and that was that.

'But we continued to grieve for him and would send him little messages mentally, in case he were "around" somewhere.

'Then I had this experience. I was barely awake, but what had awakened me slightly was the feeling that I was lying on top of a cat, with my arms holding him very close to my chest. I could feel him purring and hear him purring. The vibration of the purrs was resonating in my chest and his purrs were continuous and fairly high-pitched, of a kind he always gave when he was deliriously happy. I didn't know how I could be lying on top of him, although I do tend to, and was lying on my stomach, but that made it seem impossible anyway. But there he was. At least, I assumed it was Sam.

'But as soon as it became apparent to me that I was hugging this cat tightly to me, and it was an unmistakable sensation, one that I couldn't deny or put down to illusion, I immediately began to question the identity of the cat. Was it Tara or Sam? I kept trying to answer that question but the more intently I asked the question and tried to work out which cat it was, the fainter grew the purrs and I felt him or her diminishing and fading away. The experience lasted for about twenty seconds, I would estimate.

'I was awake then and woke my wife and told her.

There is no question in my mind that it was not a dream. It was too physically real and even today I can recall the sensation of the purring vibrating against my chest. Since that day, as a consequence of this "visit", I have been reading books on life after death and it has completely reoriented my consciousness towards accepting survival. Perhaps Sam thought it was time my evolution was furthered and that was one way he knew of ensuring it. I now believe that we shall meet again one day and that has given both my wife and me great hope and inspiration.'[7]

Now, as with relatives and friends who appear with some sort of after-death communication pre-empting their death, encounters are the same with pets, as Sara Dann explains:

'I have a lovely story of my recently deceased cat Holly who made contact with me. While on holiday in Italy, I had a "dream" about her – she was somehow at a crossroads, a place very green and with two paths to go down. I can only describe this place as a green square with leafy avenues leading off it, like a London park.

'A faceless stranger was trying to get her down one path and she resisted, looking at me, and saying, "It's OK, I know which way to go." I reassured her and off she went down the other path – she kept looking back at me and I kept telling her that it was OK.

'On waking up, I told my husband about this pleasant dream I had of Holly … neither of us thought any more of it.

'However, less than two hours later, a phone call from

7 Taken with permission from http://www.adcrf.org

the cattery told us that Holly had died peacefully in her sleep. At first, I was very, very upset, but Phil later said maybe it was Holly letting me know that she was going and that she went peacefully. This gave me great comfort; also, it shows how much she loved me. We talked and had a great understanding – which some people think stupid. However, I know differently.'

On a similar note, Pauline texted into one of the radio shows on which I was talking about this book to tell a tale about her cat. She was touring America some years ago and had left her cat at her son's house. When in Las Vegas, she had a really vivid dream that her cat was trapped somewhere. It was dark, he was hyperventilating and in a panic and she was trying to fly back to rescue him. When she woke, the dream would not leave her so she phoned her daughter who lived in San Francisco and told her. She rang her brother and he said they had been up half the night as the cat had gone missing. After another day he turned up very upset and with his claws all worn away. Obviously he had been trapped and was trying to claw his way out! Telepathy must work long distance!

PETS RETURNING TO SAY GOODBYE

I have read and received other accounts where beloved pets have returned from the grave at the passing of their owners. One such example read:

'When my father was posted with the British Army to Germany in the late 1940s he found himself an Alsatian

dog, whom he called Asta. At first, the tour was unaccompanied, but then my mother joined him and two years later I was born, so I grew up in Germany with Asta. Sadly, she had to be put to sleep some time later and we came to England. In 1991, my father passed away but while my mother and I were sitting by his bedside in the hospice, I saw Asta come and sit with me, as if waiting for my father to take her home. This was nearly forty years after she had gone to heaven.'[8]

Franklin D. Roosevelt was given Fala, a Scots Terrier pup, as a gift from his cousin Margaret. He and his master became inseparable. Fala accompanied him everywhere, eating his meals in Roosevelt's study and sleeping in a chair at the foot of his bed. He became witness to history and during the last week of December 1941, twenty -six nations at war with the axis had negotiated a declaration of unity and purpose. The document was signed in the President's study with Fala stretched out on the carpet asleep and snoring gently!

The Secret Service of the day would try as they might to keep the president's trips secret. However, two things always gave the game away! One was the ramp that had to be installed for his wheelchair and the other was the presence of Fala! They could sometimes dispense with the ramp but certainly not Fala! The sight of a little Scottie dog was a dead giveaway to the nearby presence of their leader. Little wonder then that the Secret Service gave Fala a code name. He was known as 'The Informer'.

On D-Day, during a White House press conference, Fala was

8 *Fairy Tales* – Spring Equinox 2006. Issue 28, p. 18.

seen running free through the Oval Office. He had Roosevelt well trained – feeding was a ritual. No one other than the President was allowed to feed the little Scottie. You had to hand the bowl to the President and he would feed Fala out of his own hand! No matter who you were, everyone had to wait for their own supper until the little dog dined!

President Roosevelt died in 1945 and was buried on 15 April. West Point cadets raised their rifles and gave the customary three volleys. After each volley, a friend of Eleanor Roosevelt noted that Fala barked, a child whimpered and then it was over. The little Scottie – who had been the constant companion of one of the world's great leaders rode on his master's funeral train from Warm Springs to Washington. Now five years old, he attended the burial services in New York State's Hyde Park with the very person who gave him to Roosevelt as a pup! Fala cowered and whimpered at the gun salute and rolled on the grass during the hymn. He barked furiously at the gun volleys but was led away quietly at the end.

Readjustments had to take place which were especially difficult for Eleanor Roosevelt. She observed that her husband's little dog never got used to losing the President. When a car came down the drive of their home accompanied by the wailing of sirens, Fala's ears pricked up, his legs straightened out and she knew the little dog was expecting to see his master!

Fala accepted Eleanor after her husband's death but it seemed as though he felt that she was just someone to put up with until his master's return. Some dogs forget; Fala never did. Whenever he heard the sirens, he always became alert and one supposes he felt again that he was as important then as in former times.

Although initially parted after the funeral, Fala was eventually reunited with Eleanor Roosevelt and they became inseparable. They went on long walks through the woods together and he sat beside her chair in the living room and greeted her whenever she returned home. Still, Fala missed the President! He never gave up hope of seeing his master coming down the drive.

The little Scottie died in 1952 and he was buried near Roosevelt in Hyde Park, New York. A statue of him can be seen at the feet of the President at the FDR Memorial in Washington, D.C.

One of my favourite animal ADC experiences features Thor, a beautiful white swan. Marilyn Evans is well known as an animal healer in the West Country. At the time, she ran a small wild bird and animal hospital where Thor was taken in. He was badly covered in oil, with an injured leg, and had lost his beloved mate:

> 'It took just an hour to make contact with him and gain his confidence and he allowed me to stroke him. His response was to put his neck around mine and totally relax. We were friends! After that, I cleaned him in our bath. Thor wandered around the garden during the day; at night, I tucked him under my arm, carried him upstairs and he bedded down in the bathroom, quietly "talking" and honking to me.
>
> 'After nine months, Thor decided it was time to return

to the wild ... he was released on the Tamar at Moditonham Quay, near Saltash, where he was first rescued and brought to us. Through the local Sunday Independent and various contacts I found he had "emigrated" over to Torpoint in Cornwall.

'One Christmas Eve at 10pm, we had an urgent police message – a swan was in trouble at Torpoint. My husband Dennis and I immediately drove over there but all the swans seemed to be all right. Three days later, another urgent message came and this time I found Thor lying on the beach – he was in a terrible state, unable to hold his head up fully and breathing with great difficulty. He'd been washed in and out by the tide for days ...

'Gathering him in my arms, I placed his soft neck around mine and we all drove home in quietness. I knew the earthly end was near for him. The following evening, at ten o'clock, Thor quietly and peacefully died in my arms ...

'One evening, four years later, I was stunned to find Dennis had quite suddenly left his earthly body, too, sitting in his chair just minutes after we had been talking about animal healing.

'At his semi-military funeral, the weather was grey and drizzling. After the service, we came to the graveside unable to see more than a few yards through the gloom.

'A bugler sounded the "Last Post" and, as the last, deeply moving notes died away in the still air, a shaft of light lit up the scene. I felt a sudden sense of awe. Three mourners asked me if I had seen the extraordinary beam of light. Each described "a swan with outstretched wings". That is why a swan is carved on Dennis's headstone.'

Animals also react around the dying – one phone call to a radio show was from a milkman, Malcolm telling me about his friend who worked as a postman. Each day, they would have a cup of tea together at Malcolm's early before work. Malcolm's dog never barked at his friend as he knew him well, but one morning, for seemingly no reason, the dog were berserk, barking and sniffing around him and just wouldn't let up. Neither of them knew what had got into him and so they chuckled and went off to work. Next morning his friend never arrived for a cup of tea he had died that night in his sleep … Did the dog know?

One radio show Chris called me to share the tale of when she was dog-sitting for her uncle in Bournemouth. One evening, the dog stood up and let out an incredible howl, which was totally out of character and a noise she had never heard it make before. An hour later, she received a call from another relative with some bad news – her uncle had died, at exactly 6pm when the dog had got up and made the odd noise.

The experience Ray Grindell had describes the reaction of his dog the moment his grandmother passed away. One can only wonder what the animal sensed. As explored in my last books, I wonder whether this counts as evidence that something occurs the moment we take our last breath – perhaps the dog felt Ray's grandfather coming to collect his wife, or was the dog aware of her spirit leaving her body?

'I was sixteen and living with my parents and widowed grandmother … my grandfather, George, had died a few years earlier. My grandmother became critically ill and was being nursed by my mother in an upstairs bedroom. My mother would sit at the bedside of my grandmother with our pet dog, Blackie, a Cocker Spaniel, for company. I must stress that Blackie was absolutely fearless, be it of humans or other animals.

'On this particular evening, my father and I were sitting downstairs in the lounge listening to the radio when we heard something rushing down the stairs, whining and howling. As we opened the door, Blackie rushed in with all the hair standing up on his back, and he rushed under the table, whining and cowering, and was absolutely petrified. My father then called out to my mother, who was still upstairs and she then related what had happened.

'As she was sitting at the bedside, my grandmother came out of the coma she was in, lifted her head from the pillow and, without any sign of illness, gave a brilliant smile, looked up to the corner of the room and said, "Hello, George," and at that second passed away. At the same second, Blackie who was laid at my mother's feet, shot up and looked in the exact place where my grandmother had looked, and with absolute terror and hair on end, whining, shot out of the room and flew down the stairs to my father and me.

'I am convinced that both my grandmother and Blackie had seen an angel that had come down for my grandmother in the guise of my grandfather.'

SYMBOLS AND ANIMALS

As described in my second book, *After-Death Communication*, not all after-death communications are visions, voices or scents – some are more subtle. The bereaved frequently wish or will a higher power, the universe, or their deceased loved one (human or animal) to give them a sign that he or she still exists and, indeed, that they are all right. Many receive such a sign, though it may take some time to arrive. Occasionally, these signs are so subtle they may be missed, or they can be discounted as mere 'coincidences'.

It is worth mentioning here that messages are also believed to be conveyed through natural symbols: rainbows, butterflies, birds and animals, or via the unexpected movement of physical objects. Any of these inexplicable happenings may occur shortly after the death of the loved one, or months or years later.

BUTTERFLIES

In ADCs butterflies crop up again and again and I had not realised the close relationship they had with death. Perhaps because of their metamorphosis from an earth-bound caterpillar to a stunning airborne butterfly they are used as a symbol for personal growth and spiritual rebirth, and have more recently been seen as a spiritual symbol for life after death. Just walk into any nursery, hospice or hospital and you will find pictures of butterflies. This symbol is also used extensively by many grief counsellors, spiritual and religious centres, and support groups for the bereaved.[9]

One well-documented account is of Bill Rosenberg[10], who described how, as the casket containing the body of his wife, Julie, was being lowered into the ground at the cemetery, a huge

9 Guggenheim, B. and J., *Hello from Heaven*, Bantam USA, Ch. 14

10 on the *Sally Jessy Raphael* show, syndicated 1 December 1989; topic: I Was Too Young To Lose My Wife

yellow butterfly flew up from the bottom of the grave. It flew over to Bill, then passed by several other family members, resulting in each of them feeling uplifted by their special experience.

Dawn McCoy-Ullrich wrote about her father-in-law who passed away in September 1989:

> 'My husband and I, along with his sister and brother, were all camping on the Father's Day weekend, the year following his death. We were moping around talking about Papa and how much we missed him. In the afternoon, we all retired to our tents for a nap. When we woke up, the entire sky and ground around us was covered with yellow-and-black butterflies. There were literally hundreds of [them]. It was positively ethereal, as if we were not on earth but somewhere else. This was an incredibly spiritual experience for us and, for years after, we often wondered why this happened. Were the butterflies a sign?'[11]

Another instance concerned a lady who lived all her life in a village in Kent where she became a devoted servant of her parish church and other neighbouring churches, and where she was the organist. A few years ago, this lady died, having previously assured her friends that when her time came, she would return as a butterfly. At her funeral, everyone noticed that during the vicar's eulogy there was a butterfly in the church, fluttering near, and it later disappeared. Much later at a neighbouring church where this lady used to play, a butterfly appeared as well. The organist used to take special

11 Taken from http://www.canoe.ca/LifewiseHeartSoulwise00/24 May 2000

pride in her instrument, which was a fairly old and not-too reliable harmonium that one had to pedal. She would always insist that fresh flowers were placed upon a special stand nearby at services. To this day, the harmonium remains temperamental. Yet now, it always works when fresh flowers are placed on the stand, and on three recent occasions has broken down when they are not, leaving the service to continue without it.

A friend also told me about an experience which happened at a funeral she attended:

'Hilda reminded me for all the world of the character in the children's book Mrs Pepperpot. Her tiny frame and crab-apple cheeks made one smile and, although her face was creased with age, her eyes still twinkled. At the age of ninety-two, she told me that she was 'ready to go' and had all the funeral arrangements organised, even down to the food the mourners would eat. She stood at only 4 feet 10 inches tall and yet was strong in body and mind, having worked hard all her life and [she] brought up her family alone after the early death of her husband. Here she was in the twilight of her years, as strong-minded and cheerful as ever, ready to fly to the next world, as she put it.

'Eventually, she began to grow weaker and was confined to bed for only a short time before she died in her sleep. The day of her funeral had an atmosphere of celebrating her life rather than mourning. It was a cold, sunny November day when Hilda's tiny, flower-laden coffin was carried into the beautiful old church. The

church was chilly and, as the sun was behind the clouds, the mourners shivered a little. The vicar had known Hilda well and spoke of their long association and how cheerful and welcoming she had always been. It was a beautiful service, which culminated with words from the vicar who said that he was sure that, at that moment in time, Hilda's soul was on its way to heaven. At precisely that moment, the sun broke through the clouds and poured through the stained-glass window directly onto the little coffin. It directed its beam like a spotlight. From the depth of the flowers resting on the coffin, something stirred and a huge, beautiful moth flew directly up inside the ray of light. It was one of those symbolic moments that stay in the memory forever.'

Joan Silberglied lost her younger brother Robert in the 1982 Air Florida Flight 90 tragedy which clipped the Fourteenth Bridge and plunged into the icy waters of Washington's Potomac river, leaving just five survivors. Twenty-one years on, Jean remembers that 'on the day of his funeral, I went outside my parents' condo for a cigarette. The grounds were almost desolate, but as I sat there a small yellow butterfly came up out of nowhere and hit me in my face. As it fluttered away, these words formed in my mind: "Bye, Bob."[12]

After his eighteen-year-old son Matt died very suddenly of bacterial meningitis, Bob Pano's daughter Penny had a symbolic ADC with a Monarch butterfly, which landed and

12 12/1/03 *Observer* Magazine, pp. 18–25, 12 January 2003, Dispatches – article by Emily Yoffe

stayed on her fingers for nearly half-an-hour. Later, Penny found a colour photograph of a Monarch, which Matt had given her before he died and he had handwritten his name on the back of it. These two experiences have helped this bereaved family enormously.[13]

Similarly, in August 1999, when another Boxer belonging to Barbara Gilbert died, she told me, 'I saw her spirit leave her body. The only way I can describe it, it looked like a white butterfly with its wings closed. One night last year, I was in bed watching TV (it was late, so it was dark) ... I saw a white butterfly outside my bedroom window. It was Rummie (that was her name) come to let me know she was all right.'

Finally, Roger Butler's letter read:

'I would like to relate two experiences I had – one following the death of my wife and the first experience about seven days before her death, on each occasion concerning the appearance of a Red Admiral butterfly.

'My wife was terminally ill and, seven days before her death, while I was sitting with her at the hospital bed, the window above her head was open about 6 inches and in fluttered the butterfly, circled the head of her bed, flew out of the window and then returned and repeated its performance ... This was late October 1997.

'The second experience occurred two months following her death in mid-February 1998. I was tending to her grave in our local churchyard and the exact experience happened again. This Red Admiral butterfly quite suddenly appeared, fluttered around her grave, it then

13 'Matt's Butterfly' by Bob Pano, *Bereavement* magazine, May/June 1994

fluttered off and returned about two seconds later and again circled the grave and completely disappeared.

'Certainly, on the second occasion I could not really believe a butterfly would be out on a cold February afternoon.'

Equally there are as many accounts in the same vein where people interpret robins or certain animals as being signs or symbols that their loved one is near.

To conclude, there is little doubt that such experiences closely resemble those of the human dead. As Douglas Davies writes, 'The way in which the death of pets fits into the overall scheme of human bereavement should not be ignored, for it affords a window into the significance relationships for particular individuals ... attitudes to the death of pets are also one way of reflecting on wider attitudes to human life and death.'[14]

So, to come full circle: are animals psychic or just super-sensitive? I will leave you, the reader, to decide. Personally, I think there are elements of both, but this depends on the individual animal. If humans can be psychic, why cannot animals? After all, they have been treading this earth far longer than us and need to rely on their instincts of survival far more than we do these days – thus their innate intelligence and ability for their senses to be finely honed are not merely for self-defence and self-preservation, but can be used in other positive ways. Even so, their impact and assistance to us mere mortals is incredible.

14 Davies, D., *Death, Ritual and Belief*, p. 172, Cassell, London, 1997

APPENDIX I

Assistance Animals

CONTACT DETAILS

Assistance Dogs (UK)

Assistance Dogs International (ADI) is a worldwide coalition of not-for-profit organisations that train and place Assistance Dogs. The objectives of ADI are to:

- Establish and promote standards of excellence in all areas of Assistance Dog acquisition, training and partnership
- Facilitate communication and learning about member organisations
- Educate the public about the benefits of Assistance Dogs and ADI membership

ADI retains a list of organisations throughout the world that are registered centres for the training of:

- Hearing Dogs
- Guide Dogs
- Service Dogs
- Therapy Dogs
- Seizure Alert Dogs

For more information, visit www.adionline.org

Assistance Dogs (UK) (AD (UK))

AD (UK) is the umbrella organisation for the registered charities training dogs for disabled people within the United Kingdom. It aims to improve access for people who depend on those dogs in places such as supermarkets, restaurants, on public transport and in other public places.

The registered charities that currently form AD (UK) are:

- Hearing Dogs for Deaf People
- The Guide Dogs for the Blind Association
- Support Dogs
- Dogs for the Disabled
- Canine Partners

Hearing Dogs for Deaf People

Launched at Crufts in 1982, Hearing Dogs for Deaf People trains and supplies dogs which alert deaf people to specific sounds, at home, in the workplace and also in public buildings. In 2006 they commissioned a study to investigate the benefits of placing hearing dogs with deaf children.

The Grange
Wycombe Road
Saunderton
Princes Risborough
Buckinghamshire
HP27 9NS

Tel: 01844 348 100 (voice & minicom)
Fax: 01844 348 101

E-mail: info@hearing-dogs.co.uk
Website: www.hearing-dogs.co.uk
Registered charity no. 293358

The Guide Dogs for the Blind Association

Founded in 1934, The Guide Dogs for the Blind Association works with the world's largest breeder and trainer of working dogs.

Hillfields
Reading Road
Burghfield Common
Reading
Berkshire
RG7 3YG

Tel: 0870 600 2323
Fax: 0118 983 5433

E-mail: guidedogs@guidedogs.org.uk
Website: www.guidedogs.org.uk
Registered charity no. 209617

Support Dogs

Dogs are trained to meet the needs of people with medical conditions such as hypoglycaemia (diabetes), agoraphobia and Ménière's disease. The dogs can help by bringing the person their medication or by getting help or pressing an alarm if the person becomes ill. Seizure Alert Dogs are specially trained to help and assist epileptics.

Disability Assistance Dogs are often the client's own pet dogs who are trained to help their owner with everyday activities. From the beginning of the training both dog and client work together to teach the dog tasks such as opening and closing doors, switching lights on and off, loading and unloading the washing machine, picking up, fetching and carrying objects. They can also be trained to help their owner dress and provide stability to people when walking.

21 Jessops Riverside
Brightside Lane
Sheffield
S9 2RX

Tel: 0870 6093476
Fax: 0114 2617555
E-mail: supportdogs@btconnect.com
Website: www.support-dogs.org.uk
Registered Charity no. 1088281

Dogs for the Disabled

Dogs for the Disabled has been training and supplying dogs for physically handicapped people since 1986.

The Frances Hay Centre
Blacklocks Hill
Banbury
Oxfordshire
OX17 2BS

Tel: 0870 077 6600

Fax: 0870 077 6601

E-mail: info@dogsforthedisabled.org
Website: www.dogsforthedisabled.org
Registered Charity no. 1092960

Canine Partners

Canine Partners assists people with disabilities through the help of specially trained Assistance Dogs.

Mill Lane
Heyshott
Midhurst
West Sussex
GU29 0ED

Tel: 08456 580480
Fax: 08456 580481

E-mail: info@caninepartners.co.uk
Website: www.caninepartners.co.uk
Registered Charity no. 803680

Children in Hospital and Animal Therapy Association (CHATA)

CHATA organise hospital visits with specially trained animals to children in hospitals throughout the UK.

87 Longland Drive
Totteridge
London
N20 8HN

Tel. 0208 445 7883

Pets As Therapy

Pets As Therapy organised therapeutic visits to hospitals, hospices, nursing and care homes and special needs schools with temperament tested and vaccinated dogs and cats.

3 Grange Farm Cottages
Wycombe Road
Saunderton
Princes Risborough
Bucks
HP27 9NS

Tel: 0870 977 0003
Fax: 0870 706 2562

http://www.petsastherapy.org/

Registered Charity No 1112194

APPENDIX II

ANIMAL ORGANISATIONS AND OTHER LINKS

Dr Rupert Sheldrake's homepage:
www.sheldrake.org

ANIMAL CHARITIES

Dogs Trust (formerly National Canine Defence League (NCDL)):
www.dogstrust.org.uk/

The Blue Cross:
www. bluecross.org.uk

The Kennel Club:
www.the-kennel-club.org.uk

DISABILITY WEBSITES

British Council of Disabled People:
www.bcodp.org.uk

Disability Information and Advice Services:
www.dialuk.org.uk

Disability Information Services:
www.disabledinfo.co.uk

Know Your Rights Guide for Assistance Dog Owners:
www.drc-gb.org

National Society for Epilepsy:
www.epilepsynse.org.uk

Epilepsy Action:
www.epilepsy.org.uk

The Good Access Guide for People with Disabilities:
www.goodaccessguide.co.uk

APPENDIX III

THE ANIMALS' WAR EXHIBITION AT THE IMPERIAL WAR MUSEUM

The Animals' War is a major new exhibition exploring the remarkable role of animals in conflict from the World War I to the present day. Visitors can find out about cavalry horses, mules, elephants, camels, horses and other creatures that have transported soldiers and equipment, often in difficult terrain; the pigeons and dogs who have carried messages; the dogs who have guarded military personnel and property, located injured soldiers, tracked the enemy and sniffed out explosives as well as the animals adopted as official and unofficial mascots and pets by the Armed Forces.

The Animals' War uses photographs, film, sculptures, memorabilia and interactive features to explore the intriguing and often surprising stories of animals in war. Among them are

Rob, the SAS dog who made over twenty parachute drops during the World War II; Roselle, the Labrador, who led her owner to safety from the seventy-eighth floor of the World Trade Center after it was attacked on September 11 2001; Rin Tin Tin, who was found as a puppy on the Western Front and went on to become a Hollywood legend; Voytek, the bear mascot of the 22nd Transport Company of the Polish Army Service Corps, who saw action at Monte Cassino in 1944; and Simon of HMS *Amethyst*, the only cat to have been awarded the 'animals' Victoria Cross', the PDSA Dickin Medal.

The Animals' War is exhibited at The Imperial War Museum London until 22 April 2007 and will then transfer to Imperial War Museuem North in Manchester in the summer of 2007.

For general enquiries, telephone 0207 416 5320/1, or see www.iwm.org.uk.

Bibliography

'We patronise them for their incompleteness, for their tragic fate of having taken form so far below ourselves. And therein we err, and greatly err. For the animal shall not be measured by man. In a world older and more complete than ours they move, finished and complete, gifted with extensions of the senses we have lost or never attained, living by voices we shall never hear. They are not brethren, they are not underlings; they are other nations, caught with ourselves in the net of life and time, fellow prisoners of the splendour and travail of the earth.'
Henry Beston on the animal world, The Outermost House, c. 1925 [1]

Ball, S. and Howard J. Bach Flower Remedies for Animals, Vermillion, London, 2005

1 With thanks to Sylvia Hickman for finding this quote

Chat It's Fate! magazine back issues.

Cumming, Tess & Wolstencroft, David *Pet Power: Amazing True Stories of Animal Bravery and Devotion*, Ebury Press, London, 1997.

Davis, Burke, *The Civil War: Strange and Fascinating Facts*, Wings Books, New York, 1960.

Davies, Douglas, *Death, Ritual and Belief*, Cassell, London, 1997.

Eckersley, Glennyce, *An Angel at My Shoulder*, Rider & Co, London, 1996

– *Out of the Blue*, Rider & Co, London, 1997

– *Children and Angels*, Rider & Co, London, 1999

– *Saved by the Angels*, Rider & Co, London, 2002

– *Teen Angel*, Rider & Co, London, 2003

– *Angels to Watch Over Us*, Rider & Co, London, 2006

– *An Angel at My Shoulder*, Rider & Co, London, 2007

Faust, Patricia L., (ed), *Encyclopedia of the Civil War*, *Historical Times Illustrated*, Harper and Row, New York, 1986.

Fairy Tales – Spring Equinox 2006, Issue 28.

Gardiner, Juliet, *The Animals' War*, Portrait, London, 2006.

George, Isobel and Lloyd Jones, Rob, *Animals at War*, Usbourne, London, 2006.

Jackson, Donna, *Hero Dogs: Courageous Canines in Action in New York*, Little, Brown, New York, c. 2003.

Jones, Peter C. *Hero Dogs: 100 True Stories of Daring Deeds*, 1997.

Katcher, A. H. and Beck, A. M., *New perspectives on our lives with companion animals*, University of Pennsylvania Press, 1983.

Lauber, Patricia, *The True-or-False Book of Dogs*, HarperCollins, London, c. 2003.

Millhouse-Flourie, T. J., 'Physical, occupational, respiratory, speech, equine and pet therapies for mitochondrial disease', *Mitochondrian* 4, 2004.

Mischel, I. J., .Pets As Therapy visits with terminal cancer patients'. Social-casework, 1984.

Presnall, Judith Janda, *Rescue Dogs San Diego*, [Calif.]: Kidhaven Press/Gale Group, Michigan, c. 2003 [Dogs with Jobs Series].

Quasha, Jennifer, *The Story of the Dalmatian*, PowerKids Press, New York, 2000 [Dogs Throughout History Series].

Royston, Angela, *Life Cycle of a Dog*, Heinemann Library, Oxford, c. 2000. ['Life Cycle' Series] [Heinemann First Library Series].

Schoen, Allen M., *Love, Miracles, and Animal Healing*, Simon & Schuster, London, 1996.

Seguin, Marilyn W., *Dogs of War and Stories of Other Beasts of Battle in the Civil War*, Branden Publishing Company, Boston, 1998.

Serpell, J., *In the Company of Animals: A Study of Human-Animal Relationships*, Cambridge University Press, 1996.

Sheldrake, Rupert, *Dogs That Know When Their Owners Are Coming Home*, Arrow, London, 2000.

– *The Presence of the Past: Morphic Resonance and the Habits of Nature*, HarperCollins, London 1988.

– *The Sense of Being Stared At And Other Aspects of the Extended Mind*, Arrow, London, 2003.

– with Fox, Matthew, *Natural Grace: Dialogues on Science and Spirituality*, Doubleday, London, 1996.

The Physics of Angels: Exploring the Realm Where Science and Spirit Meet, HarperSanFrancisco, USA, 1996.

Smith, Hélène, *Sally: Civil War Dog 1861–1865*, MacDonald/Sward Publishing Company, Greensburg, 1996.

Stefoff, Rebecca, *Dogs*, Benchmark Books, Salt Lake City, c. 2003 [Animal Ways Series]

Straede, C.M., and Gates, R.G., 'Psychological health in a population of Australian cat owners'. Anthrozoos, 1993.

Swanson, Eric, *Hero Cats: True Stories of Daring Feline Deeds*, Andrews Mcmeel Pub, Riverside, 1998.

Wilson, C. C. and Turner, D. C., *Companion animals in human health*, London, Sage Publications, 1998.

Wolff, A.I. and Frishman, W.H., 'Animal assisted therapy in cardiovascular disease', *Journal of Psychosomatic Research*, No. 49, 2000.